Raising Kids in an Age of Terror

Raising Kids in an Age of Terror

A FATHER'S STRATEGY ON THE WAR ON TERRORISM

C. Brian Silver

Writers Club Press
New York Lincoln Shanghai

Raising Kids in an Age of Terror
A FATHER'S STRATEGY
ON THE WAR ON TERRORISM

Writers Club Press
an imprint of iUniverse, Inc.

For information address:
iUniverse, Inc.
2021 Pine Lake Road, Suite 100
Lincoln, NE 68512
www.iuniverse.com

ISBN: 0-595-26398-4

Printed in the United States of America

Contents

Limits of Liability/Disclaimer of Warranty

The author and publisher of this book have used their best efforts in preparing this material and that it is accurate and free from errors. The author and publisher make no representation or warranties with respect to the accuracy, applicability, fitness, or completeness of the contents of this material. They disclaim any warranties (expressed or implied), merchantability, or fitness for any particular purpose. The author and publisher shall in no event be held liable for any loss or other damages, including but not limited to special, incidental, consequential, or other damages. The author and publisher do not warrant the performance, effectiveness, or applicability of any Web sites listed in this book. All links are for information purposes only and are not warranted for content, accuracy or any other implied or explicit purposes.

The author and publisher retain full copyrights as this manual contains material protected under International and Federal Copyright Laws and Treaties. Any unauthorized reprint or use of this material without permission in any format or medium is prohibited.

Introduction

Today is Wednesday July 3, 2002, almost ten months after the day that changed our world as we knew it...September 11, 2001. The United States Government has just issued a cautionary warning with respect to July 4th activities, asking all Americans to be "vigilant."

Not knowing what to do or exactly what that means, I contact the FBI office in Washington, D.C. and ask for instructions and information. As a parent of two small children, I'm seeking any guidance they can give me; some direction as to what I should do. The person who answers has none. She cannot even direct me to anyone who can answer my questions or provide any better information.

I then call the Israeli Consulate since Israel has dealt with terrorist threats for many years, and I ask them the same question. Surely, they will be better prepared. Again, there are no answers. As a parent, I feel angry and helpless in that moment. I have no clear direction as to how to prepare for or deal with this new and invisible threat. I am afraid that making a bad decision or no decision at all could have dire consequences for my family. Yet, no one can help me.

The world has dramatically changed since the morning of 9/11 when terrorists hijacked four American airplanes, crashing three of them into the World Trade Center and the Pentagon, while a fourth fell victim to an apparent passenger uprising and crashed into a field in Pennsylvania. More than 3000 people died that morning. So did America's sense of security...a feeling that "those things never happen here."

As a parent, and as an American, that day had an incredible impact on my life. Not only did I awaken from a false sense of security but also for the first time in my life as a parent, I became alarmed for the future that my children were about to inherit.

Just look at some of the events that have taken place since 9/11:

- Homeland security is a top (and controversial) issue as our government reorganizes to deal with the threat of terrorism.

- We suffered our first biological attack (anthrax), which shut down various government buildings and killed several people.

- National landmarks, bridges, banks, nuclear power plants, skyscrapers, power grids, and other important places are on a heightened state of alert.

- People who live within a certain radius of nuclear power plants are receiving potassium iodide to protect them from radiation should an attack take place.

- The government is considering vaccinating certain segments of the population against smallpox.

- New laws have been created making it easier to detain, search, and spy on people and their financial, computer, and other records.

- Words like "Ground Zero," "weapons of mass destruction," "dirty bombs," and "Jihad" are now part of our everyday vocabulary.

The world changed a lot that sunny Tuesday morning. Unfortunately, the hatred and fanaticism that bred the people who attacked us has not changed and represents the most dangerous threat facing us today. This "War on Terror" has been brewing for some time as our enemies have been escalating their attacks against us. For years they attacked us abroad, now at home.

We are now involved in a war like no other before it. It is a war with no boundaries. It is a war that will not be solely played out in some other country on some far away military battlefield. It is a war that that will not have a decisive victory. It is a war that will test us as parents, Americans, and as participants in the world community.

After 9/11, for the sake of my children's future, I needed to know why we were under attack. What I discovered is that this unconventional "War on Terror" is a complex mix of religious, cultural, political and economic factors. It is as dangerous as it is complex.

The patterns that I discovered, as well as our enemy's motivations, are worthy of discussion. We must understand the root causes that feed this form of militancy in order to effectively prepare for and repel these very attacks. This discussion will include ideas on how to minimize our enemy's impact and message to the masses. Examining the causes of this war in no way legitimizes terror as a (political) weapon. Understanding your enemy is a logical and proper analysis. Part of our own pre-9/11 vulnerability was the fact that we believed it would never happen here because we didn't fully understand the terrorists or their motivations.

The global reach of this unconventional war and the disastrous weapons available to our enemies make this conflict like no other before it. The fact that religion is involved only makes it more explosive and challenging. As we know, no-matter what religion, when someone believes they are acting in the name of God, reason and compromise are usually impossible.

Another complexity of this conflict is identifying the enemy. Whom do we fight? In the event of an attack against whom do we retaliate? Is our Muslim neighbor here as a "soldier" of bin Laden? Is Saddam Hussein behind this? Is Pakistan or Saudi Arabia to blame? Will bin Laden's death mean we win? Are all Muslims eager to wage a holy war against all non-believers? The transparency of our enemy makes this a war of the shadows and has the potential to pit neighbor against neighbor.

How did we get into this mess? How do we deal with fanatical hate? How do we stop someone from massive killing when they are more than willing to commit suicide in the process? How do we negotiate, if at all, with people who desire our total destruction? How will we know if we have won this war, and at what cost to our personal liberties? How do we ensure a safer world for our children?

The government tells us to be "vigilant", the level of which is to be guided by a color-coded warning system. But what does that mean? What do we do when the color changes to orange or red? Are we supposed to look for Middle Eastern men wearing trench coats during summer? Are we to refuse to fly on an airplane where women wearing burkas are on board? Are we to spy on our neighbors who read books about Islam?

In order to give these complex questions a reference point, I will discuss how we got here, the threats to our safety, and the role each of us can play in this unconventional War on Terror. In this War on Terror, our Third World War, we must be prepared to fight on many fronts…not just the military battlefield and we must all be involved. We cannot afford to be on the fence and do nothing. The stakes are just too high. While few of us today feel we have the power to change events, there is nothing further from the truth. For our children's sake, the great "silent majority" of people around the world have to take a stand to fight this hate and scourge of terror. As with all issues of this importance…we are either part of the problem or part of the solution.

This book will also offer ideas to help you as a concerned parent prevent, as well as prepare for, another attack. Our enemy is slick and patient and will likely strike again. Despite this, you need not feel powerless or vulnerable. You may not be able to enlist in the armed forces or hunt for bin Laden, but you can join the political process, assist in your community disaster-recovery efforts, and protect your family. There are definite things you can do.

My goals in writing this book are:

- to provide you with ideas to help prevent another attack;
- to help you make informed decisions;
- to help you prepare in the event of an attack;

- to affect change in some positive way on the most important issue of our time;

- to save lives; and

- to create a better future for our children.

Obviously, I don't have all the answers. I'm not an expert in terrorism. I have never worked for any law enforcement agency. I'm just a concerned father and American. Just like you, I'm seeking answers to these difficult questions. Just like you, I am very concerned about the direction of world events. Just like you, I'm concerned about my children's future.

In the end, I am offering this book to make you think and act with reason and purpose, and ultimately, be more prepared. I believe this conflict and the further damage it can cause is the most important issue of our time. Just like you, I'm a parent. Until I became a parent, I have never known such unconditional love as I have for my children. Every time I hold my son, I wonder what kind of world he will experience, what insecurities will he live under, what sort of disasters or devastation he will see. Just like you, I fear any harm to my children. Just like you, I need to know what I can do to best prepare and protect them.

Hopefully this book will provide an effective strategy to accomplish this very important objective.

1

How Did We Get Here?

Terrorism…what is it?

The experts define terrorism (and its causes) differently. Some say, "One man's terrorist is another's revolutionary." Throughout most of history, killing innocent civilians has been used as a tactic of warfare and political ambitions. Unfortunately, there's no evidence that it will end any time soon.

The U.S. State Department defines terrorism as "premeditated, politically motivated violence perpetrated against noncombatant targets by sub-national groups or clandestine agents, usually intended to influence an audience." In plain English, terrorism is the massive killing of civilians, which is political, premeditated, and directed towards getting the biggest impact. Preferably on TV!

Obviously, the targets of the attacks on 9/11 were chosen for their American symbolism. The World Trade Center represents U.S. economic strength and the emerging global economy and the Pentagon represents U.S. military strength and the emergence of the United States as the world's pre-eminent military power in the wake of the economic and military collapse of the former Soviet Union.

Terrorists come in all flavors and from every part of the world, including our own "Born in the USA" fanatics. In 1995 Timothy McVeigh killed 168 people by bombing a federal office building in Oklahoma City. Though you might not hear a lot about these groups, we have the Ku Klux Klan, the anti-government "Patriot" movement, assorted skinheads and neo-Nazis, racists, and religious radicals. While these domestic groups represent a challenge for us, the dominant threat facing us today comes from the international Islamic fundamentalist movement.

While our embassies and armed forces have been under attack by Muslim extremists over the last few years, these incidents were deemed somewhat "acceptable" in light of the dangerous world we live in. Besides, we reasoned, these attacks seldom reached our shores. Well that all changed forever when the first jet aircraft struck the north tower of the World Trade Center. That event will be forever burned into our national consciousness. We finally woke up!

In the past, terrorist tactics have included car bombings, hijackings, kidnapping, and other means to inflict damage, cause mayhem and attract attention to their causes. More recently, the Muslim extremists use of suicide as a terror vehicle has increased. It is one of the most difficult to stop. For most of us who cherish life, it is also difficult to understand. No country knows this more than Israel. Watching them, a country alert and experienced in fending off attacks, try to deal with suicide bombings on a regular basis is incredibly frustrating and a sad commentary on human progress and civilized development. Watching Palestinian mothers send their children to commit suicide bombings for their cause, and to learn that the families are then paid a sick bounty by Iraq or Saudi Arabia, is even sadder. The insanity was further demonstrated when various pictures of babies dressed as suicide bombers surfaced in the Palestinian territories.

To show you what we are dealing with, he is statement from one of the parents of a suicide bomber: "How beautiful it is to make my bomb shrapnel kill the enemy. How beautiful it is to kill and be killed…" This guy's son, 22-year old Muhammad Al-Ghoul, detonated his bomb on a Jerusalem bus killing 19 passengers and wounding 55. The father told Reuters news service that he was "very happy…He's a martyr." How's that for parental guidance!

In the Middle East, it is the parents, the educators, religious and political leaders who use their children as weapons to blow themselves up to kill others. How we treat our children is the true barometer of how far we have progressed as a civilized society. The exploitation of children around the world for military purposes shows just how far we still need to go.

RADICAL ISLAM'S WAR AGAINST THE WEST

There is no doubt that radical Islamic fundamentalists have declared war on the U.S. and the West. The "West" is usually referred to as the Industrialized World, which includes mostly the U.S., Canada, and Europe. The U.S., as the leader of the West, is the biggest target.

This war against the West has been going on for a long time. Some experts view this dispute in historical context and argue that it has going on for <u>centuries</u>. Whatever your perspective, clearly for the past 20 years we have been under constant attack by certain Islamic fundamentalists as the events below demonstrates:

- 1979: Iranian fundamentalists take U.S. Embassy personnel as hostages and declare America the "Great Satan."

- 1983: Hizballah suicide bombing of the U.S. Marine barracks in Beirut, Lebanon, kills 241 Americans.

- 1988: Pan Am flight 103, destroyed by Libyan terrorists over Lockerbie Scotland, kills 259 people.

- 1993: Bombing of the World Trade Center by Egyptian terrorists, kills six people in a first and failed attempt to bring down the World Trade Center.

- 1993: Muslim terrorists attack American forces in Somalia.

- 1996: Bomb attacks by al-Qaeda on American service personnel in Dhahran, Saudi Arabia, kills 19 American soldiers and wounds hundreds.

- 1998: Bombing of the U.S. embassies in Kenya and Tanzania by al-Qaeda, kills 253 people.

- 2000: Bombing of the U.S.S. Cole by al-Qaeda, kills 19 Americans.

- 2001: Attacks on the World Trade Center and Pentagon by al-Qaeda suicide bombers, takes more than 3000 lives.

As you can see, the attacks against us have increased in frequency and severity. Will there be another attack on U.S. soil? Most experts believe it's not a question of if, but when. We are just too big and too wide open to prevent another attack. For that reason, we cannot be lulled into complacency because (as of this writing) there hasn't been another attack on U.S. soil since 9/11.

Our enemy is extremely patient. Culturally and philosophically, they see their mission taking shape over the course of decades. For most of us who seek fast and logical solutions, this is a strange and mysterious notion. They seek an effective outcome, not quick gratification. While the enemy will choose where and when it will strike in order to have the maximum effect, we are now entering a phase that will require us to put aside our human nature of expediency and not stand down even when it appears "nothing is going to happen." In this phase, all of us will be tested.

THE PERCEPTIONS BEHIND ISLAMIC ANGER AND HATRED

While there are numerous Islamic terrorist groups and at least an equal number of splinter groups and rogue terrorist cells, it's clear that Osama bin Laden's al-Qaeda group, Arabic for 'The Base', and the terrorist network this group is trying to build, presents the most serious threat to the U.S. and the West. Since its creation in 1988, al-Qaeda's goal has been to "unite all Muslims and to establish a government which follows the rule of the Caliphs." Caliphs means "one who replaces someone else who left or died," alluding to the successor to the Prophet Muhammad's position as the political, military, and administrative leader of the Muslims. Bin Laden has stated that the only way to establish this new order is by force.

Al-Qaeda's principal goals are to: (i) overthrow all Muslim governments that are viewed as corrupt (mostly Saudi Arabia, Egypt, Pakistan, and other Muslim countries that have diplomatic relations with the West or those not strictly enforcing Islamic law); (ii) drive Western influence from those countries; and (iii) abolish state boundaries. Ultimately al-Qaeda's political goal is to establish a large Muslim Nation governed by strict Islamic law.

His goals are to construct a multi-national religious dictatorship where all diversity and freedoms are abolished in favor of a strict Islamic code of behavior. This includes the persecution or elimination of all non-Muslims. As far-fetched as these goals may sound, these ambitions have incredible global consequences. If they succeed in overthrowing Saudi Arabia, Pakistan, and Egypt, radical Islam will control much of the world's oil, oversee Pakistan's nuclear weapons, and control the most dominant and populated Arab state in the Middle East. As you can see, the stakes are too high to turn our backs on these possible results…the political consequences too devastating to ignore.

Bin Laden advocates <u>the destruction of the United States</u>, which he sees as the largest obstacle to obtaining al-Qaeda's goals. For that reason, since 1996, he has been waging war on us. In February 1998, bin Laden announced the creation of a *new alliance of terrorist organizations* called the "World Islamic Front for Jihad Against Jews and

Crusaders," and declared its intention to attack Americans and our allies, <u>including civilians, anywhere in the world</u>. He said:

> "The ruling to kill the Americans and their allies—civilians and military—is an individual duty for every Muslim who can do it in any country in which it is possible to do it…"

This means that America and its allies are his enemies. They have declared war on us and his followers have been called upon to kill us. For most Americans, even those who support a hard line in the war on terrorism, the reasons for this hatred of the United States remains a mystery that is difficult to comprehend.

So what are the political, economic, and religious issues which fuel this hatred and why do so many Muslims connect with his message? Islamic terrorism, supported by various Middle Eastern states and other groups, is not random violence and killing. There are clear political, economic, and religious goals and motives.

Why should we care about these underlying issues and perceived grievances? Do you first ask someone "why" before he or she tries to kill you? Of course not! However, in this unconventional war on terrorism, our efforts must not only include military battles but also concerted action against the extremist's message of religious intolerance, hate and political violence in order to influence those people who are willing to follow him.

We can only wage (and win) this kind of war if we understand "why." Failing to address the root causes of Islamic terrorism, failing to deal directly and forcibly with the states and organizations that support these groups, is like killing a weed without touching the root. It eventually grows back taller and stronger. But with those root causes addressed and with support and supply lines from radical states (Syria, Iran, Libya, Sudan, Saudi Arabia and Iraq) that support these groups severed, it's inevitable that the main forces shaping Islamic terrorism will fade and eventually die.

An enlightened military, economic and political policy that addresses the root causes of terrorism is urgently needed. Policies that seek to accomplish what the U.S. and its allies have always accomplished in other lands, like the promotion of freedom and human rights, the eradication of disease, improvements in education, the building of public works infrastructures, agricultural and governmental assistance from the Marshall Plan in rebuilding Europe through the

Peace Corps of the 1960s and beyond, will begin to address the social ills that are often blamed on the West, while helping to spread an understanding of our vision of a world in which all nations have a right to peaceful coexistence. In the end, this conflict will not be won solely by missiles and tanks, but equally by words and deeds. We cannot hope to succeed without directing those words and deeds where they will do the most good in much the same way that a forward observer directs artillery to a specific target.

It is both easy and naïve to suggest that all we need to do is to understand our enemy and their grievances, have an enlightened foreign policy, and send millions of dollars and thousands of Peace Corps volunteers to the Middle East and our problems will be over? Unfortunately, in the real world where cultural, political and religious differences compete for power and resources, it will take more than that. Much more. For one thing, while peaceful overtures may be welcome by enlightened leaders of some Middle Eastern countries, we will always be dealing with countries that view us exclusively and unbendingly as the enemy. Any and all negotiations will be impossible. Even some of our so-called Arab friends will not welcome democratic changes in their country, as it would undoubtedly force them from power.

Taking a lesson from history, in much the same way we defeated the Axis powers in WWII, we must follow a hard line in foreign and military policy with regard to these countries and the groups they support. We must do what we have to do to protect *our* state, *our* people, and *our* children. While our foreign policy has not always been benevolent and fair, we need not apologize for anything. For in truth, we did not start this fight.

As we enter the 21st century, we find ourselves as the sole military superpower and leader of the free and industrialized world. We are tackling a new threat, an enemy that seeks unconventional means to kill, terrorize and defeat us. Just as we couldn't negotiate with Hitler sixty years ago, we will not be able to negotiate with this enemy. Their distortions of common decency, genuine and reasonable political objectives, and rational thought are totally absent. It is impossible to negotiate with madmen who subjugate women, seek religious dictatorship, use children as weapons, and cherish death.

Anyone that can plan mass killing of innocent woman and children can only be defeated by force. It is the only language they understand. We must be prepared to fight, using any and all means at our disposal. And because they seek nothing less than our total destruction, we must take the fight to them and destroy them first. As President George W. Bush stated in his speech to Congress in the weeks following the attacks on the World Trade Center and the Pentagon:

> "Freedom and fear are at war. The advance of human freedom—the great achievement of our time and the great hope of every time—now depends on us."

DADDY: WHY DO THEY HATE US?

The 9/11 terrorists were all Muslim Arabs. Ironically, the majority of them came from Saudi Arabia, a U.S. ally. As they say in my neighborhood, "What's up with that"? "Why do they hate us?" asked my oldest son right after the attacks. It is a question with no easy answers.

In the wake of the attacks, many of us asked…What did we do to cause such hatred that they would want to kill so many innocent people? Why were Palestinians dancing in the streets after the attack? Why have so many Pakistani mothers named their newborn sons "Osama?" Why did even the Kuwaitis, whom we helped liberate after the Iraqi invasion, believe that we deserved the attack? Why are we at war with certain Muslims and particularly Muslim Arabs? Why are they at war with us?

To understand why we are at war with radical Islam we would need to understand:

- how economically and politically devastated the Arab states are.

- how Islam is intertwined with politics.

- the different ideologies of the various sects of Islam (e.g., the Sunnis, Shiites, Wahhabis, etc.).

- the history of how the modern Arab states were created after the fall of the Muslim Ottoman Empire.

- the rise of European colonialism in the Middle East and Persian Gulf after World War I and the European retreat after World War II.

- how the politics of oil have governed relations with Middle Eastern states.

- how America is perceived and represented to the Arabs in schoolbooks, religious mosques, and in the press and TV throughout the Middle East.

There are many scholarly resources available that can shed light on these complex issues. (See Appendix II at the end of the book for some of these resources). While you can agree or disagree, here are some of the perceptions as to why we are hated so much in the Muslim Arab world.

1. While America's ideals are admired, American foreign policy has been inconsistent and anti-Muslim. For example:

    - In most Arab states there is no real democracy or economic justice, yet America says or does nothing in support of the people.

    - We support repressive regimes in Egypt, Pakistan, and Saudi Arabia.

    - America's treatment of the Arab-Israeli conflict is one-sided in favor of Israel.

- The continued sanctions and new threat of war against Iraq is anti-Arab and anti-Muslim.

2. America is only concerned about oil and money, not about Muslims.

3. America, as the leader of the Western world, supported the defeat and then colonization of the Muslims, and continues to oppress them.

4. America is seen as an arrogant bully responsible for all the suffering of the Islamic nations.

5. American culture and secularism is an affront to the tenants of Islamic law.

ARE THESE GRIEVANCES LEGITIMATE?

A. *American Foreign Policy*

There is widespread perception throughout the Middle East (and the world) that US foreign policy is to blame for the hatred Muslims feel towards us. The Arabic media, religious schools and organizations, as well as various governments we support in the region fuel these perceptions.

To blame the U.S. for their problems is completely misguided and overlooks the failures and shortcomings of their own leaders and systems of government. It also overlooks nearly two decades of U.S. attempts to address the issues central to territorial, political and religious disputes and to achieve a lasting peace in the region.

Today's Arab governments have blamed their plight on any number of external culprits, from Western imperialism to the Jews. As Bernard Lewis, emeritus professor at Princeton University and a great historian and interpreter of the Near East believes, the Arab states must instead commit to putting their own houses in order: "If the peoples of Middle

East continue on their present path, the suicide bomber may become a metaphor for the whole region, and there will be no escape from a downward spiral of hate and spite, rage and self-pity, [and] poverty and oppression." {See: *What Went Wrong: Western Impact and Middle Eastern Response*, by Bernard Lewis}

But that is not to say that claims of a misguided American foreign policy are completely without foundation or substance. Whether these grievances are perceived or real, they do exist. For us to ignore them would be equally misguided.

America reluctantly became the West's sole superpower after World War II. Before that time, we were not concerned with becoming the leader of the free world. After WWII, in our overriding obsession with containing Communism and having sufficient oil to run our economy, we sometimes aligned ourselves with corrupt groups and regimes. In doing so, we not only turned a blind eye to those who violated our own philosophy of human rights and democracy, but also to millions of Muslims and their political and economic aspirations. This sowed the seeds of conflict between the U.S. and a large part of the Muslim world. It created a still unresolved conflict between our own view of American Democracy and how we were viewed by a large majority of the Arab world who, in their view, we had mistreated in our rush to guarantee the supply of oil at any cost. In a weird sense, we were in the view of the Muslim Arabs, a country that would do business with the Devil to procure oil. In the process, we became the Devil to them.

Besides the politics of oil, our overriding obsession with containing Soviet expansion forced our alliance with repressive regimes around the world, as well as guerrilla movements that did battle against the Soviet Union. Ironically, this has come back to haunt us. We supported bin Laden and many of the terrorists we now are fighting during the Soviet war in Afghanistan. Our support and installation of the Shah in Iran in 1979 led to the world's first radical Islamic government that twenty-three years later represents a substantial threat to instability in the region and the world.

Today, our support of repressive governments in the Middle East in the name of the War on Terror is a continuation of this dangerous policy. Many people in the region view their government as so authoritarian that peaceful political change, rather than armed struggle using terror as a weapon, is not possible. We continue to end up in bed with hated and despised governments whose people blame us for their government's very existence.

To make matters even worse, while we support many of these governments, they are actively engaged in promoting hatred of us. Why? Because it provides an outlet for their religious fanatics and diverts public anger away from them. Immediately after the events of 9/11, Egypt's independent weekly al-Maydan reported, "Millions across the world shouted with joy: 'America has been hit.' This call expressed the sentiments of millions whom the American master had treated with tyranny, arrogance, bullying, conceit, deceit, and bad taste." This is from a country to which we have provided billions of aid each year!

And our longtime friend Saudi Arabia represents an even greater problem. The July 30, 2002, issue of Time Magazine noted that many Saudis fought against us in Afghanistan alongside the Taliban and that their money has funded anti-American terrorist groups, Palestinian suicide bombers, and radical schools worldwide that foment Islamic militancy. Even though bin Laden seeks to overthrow the Saudi government, the Saudi rulers made a deal with the religious zealots that effectively gives them control over social aspects of society while ignoring, and sometimes participating in, the exportation of Islamic fundamentalism. In exchange, the ruling Saudi family was to be left alone.

How can we stand by and allow our so-called friends, whom we support economically and militarily, talk out of both sides of their mouth? How can we tolerate this behavior? We have ignored this problem for too long.

Democracy, political freedoms, and human rights are what this country stands for. Our foreign policy should reflect these notions of decency and concern about the people of the world. To be true to our ideals and what we represent to the world, we need to be much more proactive in promoting meaningful change in these countries to support democracy, educational reform, human rights, and economic justice. In that way, our foreign policy will reflect who we are and what we stand for.

B. *The Arab-Israeli Conflict*

Trying to solve the Arab-Israeli dispute is a monumental task. Former president Jimmy Carter won the Nobel Prize in 2002 for his efforts dating back to the mid-1970s. Most of us would agree that Carter's goal of peace in the Middle East is no closer today than it was when Camp David accords were signed. In fact, to many, they seem even more elusive than ever.

However difficult the task, we must continue to follow this path. The U.S. is the only power broker who has the ability to do so. While the Arab-Israel crisis is not the reason that we are at war with Islamic radicals, there is probably no more rallying issue for the Arabs. They see Israel as a U.S. puppet that uses American weapons to kill their Arab brothers…the Palestinians. They see constant images of Israeli occupation and are reminded of the humiliation of four lost wars since the 1948 establishment of Israel.

However, we must not forget that the Palestinians have never been pro-Western and they have certainly never had any love affair with the U.S. They aligned themselves with Nazi Germany in World War II, the Soviets during the Cold War, and Saddam Hussein in the Gulf War. Before al-Qaeda, it was the Palestinian Liberation Organization (PLO) that provided training and weapons to most of the world's terror groups. Instead of punishing this behavior, the United Nations granted the PLO diplomatic status as the true representative of the Palestinian people. This effectively legitimized the use of terror as a political weapon, which has only exacerbated the problem.

Many Palestinians celebrated and danced in streets after the 9/11 attack calling America "the head of the snake." And a recent poll found that almost 80% of Palestinians would support Saddam Hussein again if the U.S. launches renewed military action against Iraq. Ask yourself, have you ever seen a peace march in the Palestinian territories?

The historical position of Israel unrecognized diplomatically over the decades and "at war" with most of its neighbors makes it extremely difficult, if not impossible, to negotiate with adversaries bent on destroying them. Despite a reasonable proposal to settle the conflict made at Camp David just before President Bill Clinton left office, the Palestinians not only rejected the compromise, but instead intentionally unleashed the second intifada (uprising) that has produced the current dangerous state of affairs.

Even after the Oslo Peace Agreement in 1993, terrorism and Arab statements for the destruction of Israel never stopped. The Oslo agreement gave both sides a real opportunity to show whether they truly desired peace. The Israelis could have shown more restraint in building settlements in the disputed territories after Oslo, but they did agree to give up land for peace and to the right of self-determination for the Palestinians.

On the other side, the Palestinians never implemented what was promised nor stopped speaking about eventually taking back all of Palestine. It seems that many Palestinians don't want to compromise or make peace with Israel. Compromise would be giving in to the enemy and giving up the greater goal of taking back all of (former) Palestine. Instead of going back to the negotiation table, the Palestinians unleashed the new wave of suicide attacks. It now seems clear that the Palestinian leadership under Arafat has used peace initiatives only as a disguise towards their real goal…the destruction of Israel. After 50 years, the Arabs have still not accepted Israel's right to exist. Until that changes, the chance for peace is very slim.

So where are we now? The economic destruction and human suffering that the new intifada has caused the Palestinians makes it difficult to understand how the uprising or the continued suicide bombings have helped their cause. People are not able to travel freely. Unemployment is rampant. Food is scarce. Children are becoming malnourished. But this conflict defies logic. Prompted and funded by radical Arab states, hate now permeates every aspect of the lives of many Palestinians and has caused a similar unbending suspicion and hatred on the part of their Israeli foes.

This hatred is so intense that compromise, even if it were seen as a path to political and economic improvement, would never be acceptable because it would represent surrender to a "Zionist enemy." For this reason, the past two years of the intifada have all but silenced the moderate elements on both sides.

Unfortunately, various groups that use terrorism and the killing of civilians as their main political weapon have led the Palestinians. The PLO, Islamic Jihad, Al Aqsa Martyrs Brigades, Hamas, and other fringe groups, represent a global terror network funded and supported by Iran, Iraq, Syria, Saudi Arabia, other Gulf States, private benefactors, and Muslim charities through out the world…including here in the U.S. These groups are as dangerous to world peace as al-Qaeda because they have the same underlying radical fundamentalist philosophy. A Palestinian state controlled by any one of these groups would be a nightmare for the West and the U.S.

Hamas, which is responsible for numerous suicide bombings, including one at Hebrew University that killed 5 Americans, mixes nationalism and religious fundamentalism. Its founding charter pledges to carry out armed struggle and work for the destruction of Israel with an Islamic state over every inch of Palestine. Hamas has carried out suicide bombing attacks against hundreds of innocent people, including those at a birthday party for a 13-year-old girl, a Passover celebration, a pizza shop, and shopping malls.

While these groups argue that they have no other weapon against the stronger Israeli military, killing innocent and unarmed children is the ultimate cowardly act. To confirm their depravity, the leaders of Hamas and other terror groups only send other children to carry out suicide bombings…never their own!

Palestinian leaders have consciously incorporated the culture of terrorism into their society. That's one reason why polls indicate that more than 75% of the Palestinian population favor suicide bombings and why Palestinians accord rock star status to suicide bombers who die a "martyr's" death. It's a constant message that legitimizes hatred, death and the continued suicide of children.

With so much hatred and so many "outsiders" involved in this conflict, it's clear that the parties alone are unable to stop the cycle of violence. Whenever the moderates approach even the framework of an agreement, the radicals on both sides and their outside supporters resort to violence to prevent any successful outcome. Only when these elements are removed we will have a chance for peace. Most experts argue that we must take action to neutralize the radical elements before even more catastrophic attacks take place or a war in the Middle East sets off a chain of world events whose consequences could be dire.

While we must not stop our efforts, however difficult the situation, we should also realize that redressing the grievances and dealing with the hostility of centuries of conflict are not going to happen overnight. In this regard, we may need to achieve interim agreements while adopting our enemy's patient view of world history and seek a peace that may be achieved not in days or months or even years, but in decades. In the meantime, at a minimum, we should insist that:

1. Israel gives up its claim on most of the settlements in the occupied territory.

2. Israel give back some of occupied territories in exchange for the dismantling of the terror groups in Gaza and the West Bank and an end to the goal of Israel's destruction.

3. A wall or fence on the West Bank should be constructed faster to separate the parties for a "cooling off period."

4. The U.S. should make it clear that it will not tolerate the destruction of Israel and should guarantee its existence.

5. We need to work harder to identify and support moderate Palestinians who are willing to negotiate and accept Israel as a neighbor.

6. As a matter of policy, any U.S. funds sent to the Palestinians must go towards public service and infrastructure projects, and not be available to support corrupt political regimes or to purchase weapons.

7. Syria, Iran, Iraq, and Saudi Arabia should be warned that continued assistance and support for terrorist groups are cause for economic and diplomatic isolation and possible military action.

We have to understand that only by eliminating terrorism from the equation will we have a hope of resolving the Arab-Israeli conflict.

C. *Iraq and State-Sponsored Terror*

As of this writing, the United States Congress has authorized the President to conduct military operations against Iraq and UN weapons inspections are proceeding to determine whether Iraq has weapons of mass destruction. The preparation and buildup for war against Iraq is massive and it will take a miracle to avoid a confrontation.

Despite the fact that we have yet to catch bin Laden or completely stabilize Afghanistan, President Bush seems hell bent on getting rid of Saddam. Our greatest mistake was leaving Saddam Hussein in power after the Gulf War. How strange it is that the same group of people who led the first Gulf War in 1991 and kept him in power (Dick Cheney, Colin Powell, and George H. W. Bush), are involved again to oust him…only this time it's Bush's son.

In her book *The War Against America,* Laurie Mylroie makes a compelling argument that Saddam was behind the 1993 World Trade Center bombing and is the mastermind behind international terrorism and al-Qaeda. Some people even believe that Iraqi agents were involved with Tim McVey in the 1995 bombing of the Alfred P. Murrah Federal Building in Oklahoma City.

According to government officials, Saddam is in the terrorist business, has links to al-Qaeda, and is rebuilding his chemical and biological arsenal. Vice President Dick Cheney said on August 7, 2002, that if Saddam is not stopped, "it's the judgment of many of us that, in the not too distant future, he will acquire nuclear weapons."

The war with Iraq is a difficult one because we were not attacked and many counties and a fair amount of public opinion seem to be against a new war. Kenneth M. Pollack, one of the world's leading experts on Iraq and author of *The Threatening Storm*, provides an insider's perspective on the crucial issues with respect to a new war with Iraq. Mr. Pollack, who was an analyst on Iraq for the CIA and the National Security Council, believes that the U.S. must launch a full-scale invasion to eradicate Saddam's weapons of mass destruction, and rebuild Iraq as a prosperous and stable society—for the good of the world. This is because if Saddam possesses nuclear weapons he will return to his stated goal of dominating the Gulf region and ultimately he will pose a greater risk than confronting him now. We appear to be entering a period of foreign policy where preemption, in lieu of deterrence or containment, might become the standard.

It appears to me that President Bush sees Iraq in moralistic terms. They are evil and we must destroy the "Butcher of Baghdad" and liberate the Iraqi people and bring democracy and freedom to the Middle East. Bush sees Iraq in much the same way as Ronald Regan saw Eastern Europe under Soviet control. Once democracy and freedom is introduced into the area, it will have a domino effect on the entire Middle East. Only then will the Arab states truly join the free world.

However, the issue of state and group sponsored terrorism is much bigger than Iraq. Even if we remove Saddam, what will we do when Iran, which exports radical Islamic fundamentalism, obtains nuclear weapons and can threaten the entire Middle East? The State Department says Iran is the primary state sponsor of terrorism today; it also accuses Cuba, Iraq, Libya, North Korea, Sudan, and Syria of sponsoring terrorism. President Bush has labeled Iraq, Iran, and North Korea an "Axis of Evil."

These counties use terrorism as a cost-effective way in which to wage war by proxy. For instance, Hizballah, supported by Iran and Syria, is a formal organization that has carried out numerous anti-U.S. attacks overseas; including the October 1983 bombing of the U.S. Marine barracks in Lebanon. With the exception of the al-Qaeda network, Hizballah is responsible for the deaths of more Americans than any other terrorist group in the world.

According to the Council on Foreign Relations, a U.S. nonpartisan membership organization, Syria provides training, weapons, safe haven, and logistical support to Islamic terrorist groups. The Popular Front for the Liberation of Palestine-General Command, Hizballah, and the Islamic Jihad have their headquarters in Syria, and Hamas maintains offices there. It was recently reported that Syria is allowing al-Qaeda terrorists to operate in Syrian controlled areas of Lebanon. Syria is a virtual office complex of terror groups.

Syria, Iraq, and Iran need to be completely isolated diplomatically, economically, and politically unless and until the terror networks they support and maintain are destroyed. Because no one believes that will be enough, aggressive military action should be contemplated as well. These countries should be made aware that if terrorism strikes the U.S. from any terrorist groups they support, war is inevitable, with the full brunt of U.S. military power brought to bear on them. In other words, "assured destruction."

Despite our cozy relationship with Saudi Arabia, our long time friend and ally, they are a major sponsor of international terrorism. The mosques and Saudi society produced bin Laden. This is no coincidence. It is the ironic and unintended, but inevitable, consequence of an U.S. policy that turned a blind eye to Saudi government support for radical Islam and terror. On September 11, we paid the price for that policy.

The Washington Post reported that a briefing held on July 10, 2002, for the Defense Policy Board, a group that advises the Pentagon on defense policy, depicted <u>Saudi Arabia as an enemy to the United States</u> and a backer of terrorism. "The Saudis are active at every level of the terror chain, from planners to financiers, from cadre to foot soldier, from ideologist to cheerleader," stated the briefing prepared by Laurent Murawiec, a Rand Corporation analyst. "Saudi Arabia supports our enemies and attacks our allies." He also urged the United States to demand that Saudi Arabia stop funding fundamentalist Islamic outlets around the world, and stop all anti-U.S. and anti-Israeli statements in the country. Evidence continues to surface revealing Saudi complicity in supporting and funding Islamic fundamentalism. It's about time that our foreign policy reflected a realistic view of our relationships with governments in the region, not just a reflection of relations and oil at any cost.

What's more, while the threat of terrorism also confronts other countries, some of them continue to act in a way that supports the very forces against us all. Russia, who is a prime target of terrorism from Chechnya rebels and other groups, just signed an agreement to provide Iran with nuclear technology to build nuclear power plants and has signed a multi-billion economic deal with Iraq. France is interested in supplying Iran with weapons. China and North Korea are the main exporters of weapons to many of these countries that support terrorism. China, Russia and France (all of which are permanent members of the U.N. Security Council) should be told to stop exporting weapon technology and economic assistance to terrorist states or stop trading with the U.S. Why give money and support to those who support and supply your enemies?

The world must take concerted action now against the states that sponsor terrorism or risk more attacks. Without state sponsorship, terrorists have less money, less support, less intelligence, and less places to hide.

D. *The Politics of Black Gold*

Since the oil embargo of 1973 it's incredible that we remain so dependent on Mideast oil. While that dependence has slowed somewhat, we still get a lot of our oil from that region. Twenty-five percent of the world's oil, the lifeblood of the industrialized world, is controlled by one of the world's most unstable and corrupt regimes in the region, Saudi Arabia.

Let's not downplay the importance of oil. It is the juice that drives our economy. While the political rhetoric hints at higher motives, the major reason for the U.S. entry into the Gulf War was to stop Saddam Hussein from taking control of the oil fields of Kuwait and Saudi Arabia. Considering our unending desire to drive our SUVs and the fact that we consume 25% of the world's oil, no doubt it is a contributing factor to the idea a new war against Iraq as well. Iraq is known to have substantial oil reserves and access to those reserves would slow our dependence on Saudi Arabia and loosen the noose that OPEC has on world oil prices and production.

According to the Department of Energy, the United States imports around 57% of total U.S. oil demand. Around two-fifths of this oil comes from OPEC nations, with Persian Gulf sources accounting for about one-fifth of total U.S. oil imports. Oil is, and has been for over 80 years, the dominant reason we are concerned about the Middle East. Bin Laden's goal of an American retreat from the Middle East would assure that control of the world's most strategic oil resources would fall into the hands of radical Islamic interests.

There is no denying the fact that our thirst for oil has created strange bedfellows. As long as Saudi Arabia and other Gulf States quench this thirst, provide outlets for American products and purchase U.S. Treasury notes with their oil money, we will be forced to aid and financially support the very forces that attack us ideologically, as well as physically, through acts of terrorism.

According to the CIA, while the global economy will continue to become more energy efficient, continued global economic growth, along with population increases, will drive a nearly 50 percent increase in the demand for energy over the next 15 years. Total oil demand will increase from roughly 75 million barrels per day in 2000 to more than 100 million barrels in 2015, an increase almost as large as OPEC's current production.

The answer is simple, the solution very difficult. We must spend more to find and implement alternative energy sources, not only to slow this dependence on oil, but also to enable us to break free of ultimately self-defeating relationships with nations that export both oil and terrorism. Not to mention the environmental damage caused by the burning of fossil fuels. With the same intensity and effort we used to put a man on the moon in 1969, we must challenge the American people with their spirit and ingenuity—to harness a new form of clean renewable energy.

In the past, those calls have not resonated broadly with the population at large. But today, we have new images. We have the image of the Arab states that hold oil and who at the same time are also supporting the terrorists who led to the loss of 3,000 lives on September 11. Now is the time. We can't wait any longer.

E. *Economic Injustice and Poverty*

The broader issue of economic injustice and poverty currently suffered by Muslims of the Middle East is, unfortunately, not a problem confined to the Middle East. It is a worldwide problem…even here at home. People all over the world are under great economic distress. Finding sufficient shelter, food, and clean water is a daily problem for a significant percentage of the world's inhabitants. While poverty is rising, most of the world continues to spend large amounts of money on weapons. Something is inherently wrong with this picture in the 21st Century.

In an age where one crazy suicide bomber can cause incredible damage, it may be time to examine whether large military expenditures and weaponry equate to national security. We all need to ask ourselves whether a $350 billion U.S. military budget makes us feel any more secure. While Afghanistan proved a strong military is important, could not some of this huge amount of money go towards other forms of economic and human development abroad (and at home)? The world is a dangerous place, and we should have a strong military, but at what price?

There are certain ideas that have some merit in this regard. The Marshall Plan, which provided funds to re-build Europe and Japan after World War II, might provide some sort of historical example for what happens when we use butter instead of guns. During WWII, Germany and Japan were viewed as a far greater threat and with every bit of emotional disdain in the wake of the attack on Pearl Harbor as the al-Qaeda terrorists are today. Yet, now, sixty years after the end of World War II, they are our allies and economic partners. While post WWII Japan and Germany were culturally different than the modern Arab states, these questions need to be asked in the halls of Congress and in the meeting rooms of the State Department.

Might just some of the hundreds of billions we spend on the military, and many times waste on various government projects, be better off spent in other areas? Long-term commitment to educational and economic programs in Muslim nations, and other parts of the world is urgently needed. When people have nothing, they have nothing to lose. Clearly, we have the means and the resources to reverse that cycle.

Wade Davis, an author and anthropologist, published an article in the Canadian newspaper, The Globe and Mail, on July 6, 2002, entitled *The Ticking Bomb: An Anthropologist's View on Terrorism* where he provided an interesting explanation of the social and economic inequities that exist in the world today that fuel terrorism. He noted the huge disparities that exist in the world today between the rich and the poor. For example, did you know each year Americans spend as much on lawn maintenance as the government of India collects in federal tax revenue. He suggests that we need to turn our anthropological lens upon our culture with respect to energy consumption and materialism and how this is viewed by third world countries whose people survive on less than $100 a month. He reminds us that the message of al-Qaeda finds sympathizers and followers among disaffected people throughout the world, not only among Muslim Arabs. He further explains how globalization has not brought economic justice and harmony, but rather dislocation of language and culture, poor conditions in many cities, and few opportunities for the masses to improve or to even see that any improvement in their condition is possible.

The majority of the world's poor don't want to take up arms against the U.S. or send suicide bombers to kill innocent civilians. But these economic inequities provide our enemies their necessary rallying cry to turn the poor people of the world into their allies in a cause to redress perceived economic oppression. That's why, in many countries, bin Laden is seen as Robin Hood, who gave up riches to fight the Great Satan, not as the terrorist leader who orchestrated the deaths of 3,000 innocent civilians.

The planet's growing problem of social and economic disparity, and the increasing effects of ill-distributed wealth are creating a time bomb for the rich nations. Again, as the richest of the Western nations, the U.S. is seen as the main culprit. While the United States cannot alone solve the world's poverty problems, we need to remember that battles are fought in the hearts and minds of men as much as on a military battlefield. You can win over a lot of those hearts and minds when people's bellies are full, when they have money in their pockets, and they have hope for the future. The U.S. is the world's sole superpower and the most generous nation on earth. As with freedom and human rights, on economic justice and bridging the gap between the rich and poor, we need to lead by setting an example.

F. *The Ugly American—Public Perceptions*

In most of the Middle East, the state-run media, which is indistinguishable from the government and controlled by it, helps to promote hatred and distrust in much the same way that a prejudiced parent teaches its children to hate. The media, mosques, religious schools (madrassahs), and government educational systems fan the flames of anti-American sentiment. By making America the villain, hatred is passed from generation to generation…while corruption and incompetent leadership is overlooked. To date, we have totally ignored this problem.

While the majorities of Muslims do not sympathize with bin Laden or agree with his militant ideas, he has succeeded in attracting sympathy and support in the Arab and Third World because he has been able to effectively package his message and communicate it through various forms of the media. Without an independent media in the Middle East, and a silent moderate majority to question his ideology or radical agenda, he is free to continue to spread his message effectively and build support.

This message of hate, envy, and prejudice is magnified and reinforced by today's worldwide satellite and cable communications. The Internet has also become an effective weapon in the terrorists' arsenal, increasingly used to spread the message of jihad and to recruit members into their organizations. Al Jazerra, the Arab version of CNN, constantly flashes pictures of poverty and occupation in the Middle East perpetrated by Israel and the West, and bombards viewers with anti-American and anti-Western slogans.

These messages of hate are also found in schoolbooks and religious sermons throughout the Middle East. According to the Time Magazine article on July 30, 2002, a typical passage from a sixth-grade history textbook from Saudi Arabia vows that "Arabs and Muslims will succeed, God willing, in beating Jews and their allies."

The mosques are even worse. On June 8, 2002, for example, the Palestinian Authority television broadcast a sermon by Sheik Ibrahim Madhi preaching in the Sheik 'Ijlin Mosque in Gaza which praised suicide attacks and calls for the end of Israel, the U.S., and Great Britain. And in a nationally televised address, Sheik Abd al-Rahman of Mecca of Saudi Arabia, declared that God turned Jews into "pigs and monkeys," condemned the "poisonous culture and rotten ideas" of the West, and trashed Hinduism.

Clearly the mosques, schools, and the mass media are being used to teach children across the Middle East to hate the U.S. and the West. Pictures of American corruption, Iraqi children dying as a result of the American-induced sanctions, and Palestinian youths throwing rocks against tanks in Israel, are all visions that provoke this hatred. These images and the Yellow Journalism of the region are doing incredible damage. They are perpetuating the cycle of mistrust and hatred and creating a new generation of hard line believers who will find it difficult, if not impossible, to negotiate and find any common ground with their counterparts in the U.S. and the West.

Factual distortions about world events also represent a major challenge for the West. In many of these countries, including Egypt and Pakistan, a November 2001 poll showed people believed that Israel and the U.S. were behind the 9/11 attacks just to spark hatred against Muslims! Many people in Pakistan believe the U.S. used nuclear weapons in Afghanistan and killed hundreds of thousands of civilians! While factually inaccurate, as evidenced by these events, we should be mindful that in many cases "perceptions" become "reality", especially in closed societies where there is no objective independent news reporting. If you want to change outcomes and behaviors you have to change perceptions. This change will take time and will take more than just slogans and sound bites from Madison Avenue or some government agency.

More, much more, must also be done by Muslim leaders to show that the terrorists inside their countries are not heroes…but criminals. We must join forces with the silent moderate majority of Muslims to combat these ugly and distorted messages and move toward a more tolerant dialogue based on respect and understanding. The United States went into Bosnia to protect Muslims, yet the image of our country fighting for Muslims has never had a place in state-sponsored media in the Arab world. The U.S. has a thriving Muslim population that enjoys religious freedom, and financially supports Muslim countries throughout the world. These positive messages of religious tolerance, freedom, and diversity must be communicated to alter the negative images of the U.S., which are all too common in the world today.

Interestingly, anti-American messages are not limited to Muslim countries. Europe is angry at our foreign policy initiatives on trade issues, our failure to sign the global warming treaty, terminating the anti-ballistic missile treaty, and assorted unilateral initiatives. Even South African leader Nelson Mandela got into U.S. bashing when he recently said: "If there is a country which has committed unspeakable atrocities, it is the United States of America...They don't care for human beings." To many, our image abroad is one of being a exploitative arrogant bully only interested in money who forces our style of capitalism and culture on the rest of the world. This is not the picture most Americans see when they look in the mirror.

We can't and shouldn't expect everyone to "like" us. Being the sole superpower comes with a lot of responsibilities, including having to take unpopular and unilateral actions. But instead of acting unilaterally, we should be leading the world, by acting with moral clarity, respect and fairness.

As Thomas Friedman, the famous author and New York Times reporter recently said..."while evil people hate us for who we are, many good people dislike us for what we do". And if we want to win their respect we need to be the best, most consistent and most principled global citizens we can be."

G. *Murder in the Name of God*

The religious aspect of this conflict has deep roots and is a serious challenge for all of us. In many trouble areas today like Bosnia, Chechnya, Kashmir, Palestine, Pakistan and Afghanistan, Islamic fundamentalism is gaining widespread acceptance and is playing a major role in guiding law and public policy. All over the world, countries (including Muslim nations like Egypt, Algeria, Jordan and Pakistan) are fighting daily battles with Islamic fundamentalists.

Terrorists and the countries that sponsor them are using religion as a unifying force. If we are not careful, and if we do not take immediate action to better understand and effectively address these issues, the radical elements of Islam will take control of the hearts and minds of the Muslim masses. World religious and state leaders (especially Muslims) must do more to isolate the radical elements or risk losing the silent majority to them.

Islamic fundamentalism, like other religious fanaticism, seeks to eliminate all other forms of its religion because they do not accept its strict interpretations of religious laws. When this strict and uncompromising form of belief moves into the political arena, the result is a holy war, which is viewed as justifiable at any cost because it not only seeks to eliminate the world of corruption; it is also a battle against religious heresy.

Islamic fundamentalism is a revolutionary movement against secularism, religious tolerance and differences of opinion. It states that only through battle (jihad) can the world be purified of Jews, Christians, Hindus, and any other belief system outside of fundamental Islamic law. For this reason, it is a movement without reason and one where compromise and negotiation are not possible. The militant Islamic fundamentalist movement is, because of the breadth of its reach, political ambitions, proposed targets, and the weapons it seeks to possess, is as dangerous to world peace as Nazism in the 1930's. It must be addressed with the same zeal with which the allies confronted the Axis powers in World War II.

From an historical standpoint it is important to note that for many years Islam and the states under its rule were the most powerful countries in the world with fairly advanced cultures and societies. At one time the Muslim Ottoman Empire was the most powerful state in the world and came very close to capturing all of Europe. When the Ottoman Empire collapsed, the Christian powers of Europe began to take control of many of the Muslim states of the Middle East and Persian Gulf.

The humiliation and bitterness in the Muslim world over the medieval Crusades and the fall of the Ottoman Empire still exist today. In fact, the al-Qaeda training manual references these historical events and states: "after the fall of our Orthodox Caliphates on March 3, 1924, and after expelling the Colonist, our Islam nation was afflicted with apostate rulers who took over in Muslim nations." This is obviously a reference to the fall of the Ottoman Empire when the caliphate (Muslim leader) was abolished and all members of the Ottoman dynasty were expelled from Turkey, which then became a secular state.

This mixture of religion and politics is powerful. The political and economic humiliation that many Muslims feel they suffered at the hands of European powers and their own corrupt leaders, as well as current political/religious issues like Israel's control over Jerusalem (the third holiest city in the Islamic world after Mecca and Medina) and the presence of U.S. troops in Saudi Arabia and other Gulf States, all provide ammunition for the radicals that motivates and sustains terrorists and attracts popular support.

Islam is the world's second-largest religion in the world with over a billion followers. It is also the fastest-growing religion in the U.S. While a mystery to many Americans, Islam seems to be an accepting and honorable religion. Islam preaches self-sacrifice, service to and worship of one God, prayer, responsibility to the less fortunate, forgiveness, and the importance of family. Because Islam is so foreign to Americans, it might be helpful for us to understand its origins so that we can better appreciate the millions of peaceful Muslims among us, as well as the Muslim fanatics who are bitterly opposed to the U.S. (Excellent sources on Islam are: *Islam* by Karen Armstrong and *Unholy War—Terror in the Name of Islam* by John Esposito.)

According to the Bible, Abraham had two sons, Ishmael and Isaac (Genesis 21). Ishmael became the grandfather of the Arab nation, and Isaac became the grandfather of the Jewish nation. Following other religious texts, Muhammad was a descendant of Ishmael, while Jesus was a descendant of Moses, who was a descendant of Isaac. Muslims revere Moses. It is often said there were no two prophets who were so much alike. Muslims also respect Jesus. In biblical terms, the irony is that that Christians, Jews, and Muslims are all decedents of Abraham who all believe in the same God. While I'm no religious scholar, to my knowledge Abraham's God does not teach death, hate and intolerance.

Is Islam the religion of hate and terror as some have claimed? Is it fair to judge an entire religious group by a few fanatics? The answer is an emphatic no. The very name Islam comes from the Arabic root word "salama," which means peace. Islam not only condemns terrorism and suicide missions, but also prohibits them completely. The majority of Muslims are not filled with religious hatred nor do they want to wage a holy war against all other religions.

However, there are religious fanatics who use a tortured version of Islam to wage war as a means to use their religion to achieve their political ambitions. While they claim to speak for Allah or God, in fact they use religion to disguise their real objectives...political power and control.

Consider Afghanistan under the Taliban. Once the religious fundamentalists seized control they were no better than the previous tormented rulers. They persecuted women, expelled millions to refugee camps, destroyed Buddhist statues that were hundreds of years old, exported drugs, tortured thousands, and killed indiscriminately. Even Iran, with its 20-year-old radical Islamic experiment, has failed politically. The Iranian government and the religious leaders who govern are corrupt and intolerant, according to unbiased media reports. Indeed, every day Iranians, most of who live in poverty, seem to have lost faith in the religious theocracy that rules them. As James Woolsey, former CIA Director, recently stated, "The union of mosque and state has worked no better there than the union of church and state did in Europe."

There are many people on both sides that want to dress this conflict in religious garb. They argue that it's a classic religious dispute that dates back centuries. While religion has played a major role in many wars, when in reality, despite the rhetoric, there really is no religious clash between Islam and the West. The conflict may be cloaked in religion and religion may give it incredible energy that helps attract fanatical zealots, but the real battle is just like all others. It's about power and control. The anti-modern, anti-Western Islamic fundamentalist movement is a movement that seeks power over nations, their resources, and their people so as to impose their view of how religion should be practiced and society should be run.

While the headlines focus on terrorist attacks, the really decisive battles are taking place within Muslim communities, where radicals compete against moderates and secularists for the soul of the masses. While we can do much more to support the moderates and encourage tolerance in Muslim states, Muslims themselves must conduct the real dialogue and take on the radicals from within to prevent this from turning into a religious conflict and turning the clock back on civilization and the notion of religious tolerance.

As President Bush said on September 20, 2001, to a Joint Session of Congress:

> "Its (Islam) teachings are good and peaceful, and those who commit evil in the name of Allah blaspheme the name of Allah. The enemy of America is not our many Muslim friends. It is not our many Arab friends. Our enemy is a radical network of terrorists and every government that supports them."

Further Thoughts

I felt it was important spending time discussing the political, economic and religious background to this conflict. This was not intended to be a course in history or even a complete analysis of the issues, but rather to serve as a reference point for us to get our hands around these important issues. There are clear underlying reasons for the conflict…they may not be logical or based in reality…but they exist and must be dealt with. It is also important to understand our enemy's motives and objectives. Now that we know, make no mistake about their resolve. It's not a question about their intentions; it's a question of how we will respond.

The fact that we are now the targets of a "holy war" would be at the very least ironic to the founding fathers of our country, who legislated a separation of church and state and recognized that freedom of religion was a guiding principle of most of the early colonists in America. However, the plain fact is that religious tolerance has not always been a way of life in our country. Incidents of anti-Semitism and anti-Catholicism (and now anti-Islam) have marred the history of our country. Religious bigotry has always existed here despite our attempts to create a culture of respect. This is a time to look back and, more importantly, to look forward in a new spirit of tolerance and understanding.

Looking at the world as our neighborhood, we need to teach our children to accept and respect our neighbors' differences. As the world gets "smaller," thanks to transportation and communication advances, we need them to understand that events in the far corners of the world affect everyone. We need to give them the tools to understand the tapestry of world cultures and religions in order to be better prepared to be citizens of the world in which they live, a world that is no longer confined to our city or to the boundaries of our nation.

While we have fought and killed each other over religion, land, resources, economics and political power, I have to wonder when we will finally "get it". In an era of very ugly and nasty weapons, we either make it together or fail together. Whether I like my neighbors or not, I have to deal with them. We can't build fences high enough to shut the world out and we can't ignore the neighbors that harbor our enemies who want to hurt us. Don't we each have a moral obligation to our children to promote understanding and tolerance of each other?

Shouldn't we do our best to eliminate poverty and protect the environment that sustains all future generations?

While we can't do anything about the past except understand it, we can do something about the future. Don't our children deserve this?

2

Daddy: There's Someone in Our House

Because the United States is the dominant country that virtually fills the North American continent, we always thought ourselves safe from all but the most sophisticated missile attack by another superpower. September 11 taught us that we are no longer an island that is immune from attack. Terrorist attacks can occur with or without warning. They can result in mass casualties and fatalities. They can bring shortages of critical resources, disruption of transportation systems, economic losses, and increased emotional stress.

The lesson of 9/11 will forever be a wound in our national consciousness. But what about the future? Was 9/11 an isolated incident or will we have to live under this type of threat, along with the constant warnings of another attack, for years to come? No one knows for sure, but <u>as a parent, I have an obligation to take these threats seriously.</u>

The 9/11 terrorists lived in this country for some time. They blended into our society until it was time to strike. According to an Associated Press article on July 12, 2002, intelligence officials estimate that there are at least 5,000 al-Qaeda sympathizers in the U.S. In his book *American Jihad: The Terrorists Living Among Us*, terrorism expert Steven Emerson notes that America has become home to hundreds and possibly thousands of terrorists with networks in nearly a dozen cities, from Florida to Boston to Denver to Houston. Confirming this fact, two al-Qaeda training camps were discovered in Alabama and Oregon and a "cell" broken-up near Buffalo, NY.

Europe has even more bad guys. In July of 2002, a *USA Today* article quoted Europe's new anti-terrorism chief as stating that al-Qaeda is recruiting heavily in Europe and that almost all countries in Europe have al-Qaeda-trained people and sympathizers within their borders, ready and perhaps preparing to attack.

It is disconcerting but true that our enemies are here in our country. They are waiting and planning to attack again. In fact, since 9/11, according to the FBI, they have thwarted over 100 attacks, some abroad and some here at home. They have also issued terrorist alerts for high-rise apartments, banks, government buildings and landmarks, bridges, tunnels, and shopping malls. There are probably even more warnings that were not made public. While no attacks have taken place, the government still asks that we be "vigilant."

So what are the threats to us now that the battlefield includes our turf?

A. *Conventional Attacks*

Just as Richard Reid's attempt to blow up an American Airlines flight from Paris to Miami on December 2, 2001, the kidnapping and murder of Wall Street Journal reporter Daniel Pearl, the recent killing of U.S. Marines in Kuwait, and the nightclub bombing in Bali showed, terrorists will continue to use traditional methods of violence and destruction to inflict harm and spread fear. They will continue to use knives, guns, and bombs to kill the innocent people, take hostages, and blow up buildings and vehicles. Other types possible attacks could include cyber terror against dependent computer systems, food and water poisoning, electrical and power grid sabotage, and other assorted attacks.

B. *Biological Attacks*

Before 9/11, very few people spoke about biological weapons or the risk of such an attack. We knew that the U.S. and the Soviet Union had these weapons, but they also had nuclear weapons and, for over 40 years, acted responsibly with respect to these weapons. So, what has changed?

First of all, we suffered the anthrax attack right after 9/11. Anthrax spores were sent through the mail in at least five envelopes. Some 22 cases of anthrax were reported. Five people died. The use of anthrax in the mail effectively shut down various government buildings, including congressional office buildings. To date, there have been no arrests for these attacks.

Secondly, it's obvious the public is not told everything about the risks that exist. We have to believe that the government's concern with biological threats must be based on substantial and credible evidence. Lastly, the break-up of the Soviet Union has unleashed certain rouge groups like the Russian Mafia and ex-KGB agents who can easily obtain these biological agents and have no compunction about selling it to Islamic terror groups, who certainly possess the motivation and hatred to use them.

CIA Director George Tenet testified in Congress that documents found in Afghanistan showed that al-Qaeda was pursuing sophisticated biological weapons. In fact, Mohamed Atta, the ringleader of the 9/11 attacks, sought information on leasing airplanes that were used as crop dusters. Why? Because crop dusting airplanes can be used to spread biological or chemicals agents from the air.

The bio-weapons the experts worry about most are the "Category A" list of biological threat agents as classified by the U.S. Centers for Disease Control and Prevention (CDC). This list includes anthrax, botulism, plague (also known as the Black Death or the Pestilence), smallpox, tularemia, and viral hemorrhage fevers such as Ebola. These infectious diseases cause potentially high death rates and require special action to cure and contain. An outbreak of any of them would undoubtedly trigger public panic.

Anthrax and smallpox are the most deadly biological threats and the ones most likely to be used because anthrax is easy to produce and even a small amount can cause widespread damage and smallpox because it is contagious and can cause widespread panic and death.

Anthrax

According to the CDC, anthrax is an acute infectious disease. Anthrax infection can occur in three forms: cutaneous (skin), inhalation, and gastrointestinal. Symptoms of the disease vary depending on how the disease was contracted, but they usually appear within seven days. Symptoms of cutaneous anthrax include a raised itchy bump that resembles an insect bite but within 1-2 days develops into a vesicle and then a painless ulcer, usually 1-3 cm in diameter, with a characteristic black necrotic (dying) area in the center. Symptoms of inhalation anthrax may resemble a common cold. After several days, the symptoms may progress to severe breathing problems and shock. Symptoms of intestinal anthrax are characterized by an acute inflammation of the intestinal tract. Initial signs of nausea, loss of appetite, vomiting, and fever is followed by abdominal pain, vomiting of blood, and severe diarrhea. Direct person-to-person spread of anthrax is extremely unlikely to occur.

In 1993, the Office of Technology Assessment estimated that under certain atmospheric conditions, dispersion by airplane of 220 pounds of anthrax over Washington, DC could result in over 3 million deaths.

Smallpox

According to the CDC, smallpox is a virus in whose symptoms begin 12-14 days (range 7-17 days) after exposure. The disease starts with 2-3 days of high fever and extreme tiredness with severe headache and backache. A rash usually begins about 2-4 days after the fever with a few red spots on the face and forearms and in the mouth. It then spreads to the trunk and legs. Sores might form on the palms and soles as well. By the fourth day of rash, the spots have turned to blisters (vesicles), and by the seventh day the blisters turn to pustules (blisters filled with pus). Smallpox skin sores are deeply embedded in the skin (dermis) and feel like firm round objects in the skin. The pustules form scabs by the fourteenth day. As the sores heal, the scabs separate and pitted scarring gradually develops. Most patients with smallpox recover, but death occurs in up to 30% of cases.

Smallpox is spread from one person to another by infected saliva droplets that expose a susceptible person having face-to-face contact with the ill person or with contact with the rash or scabs. People with smallpox are most infectious during the first week of illness, because that is when the largest amount of virus is present in saliva. The virus may spread through the air when the infected person breathes, talks, laughs, or coughs. However, some risk of transmission lasts until all scabs have fallen off. A patient is no longer infectious after all scabs have fallen off, usually about 3 or 4 weeks after the start of the rash.

C. *Chemical Attacks*

Various countries have used chemical agents in warfare: Germany used chlorine gas in World War I, and again in the 1930s, the Nazis used Zyklon B (hydrogen cyanide) gas to kill millions of Jews. Iraqi President Saddam Hussein gassed both Iranian soldiers and his own Kurdish minority in the 1980s. Iran, Iraq, North Korea, Libya, Sudan, and Syria (our list of terrorist-supported states) are thought to have significant chemical-warfare capabilities that they might pass along to terrorists.

Terrorists have also used these types of weapons before. In 1995, members of the Japanese terror group Aum Shinrikyo used Sarin gas in the Tokyo subway, killing 12 people and injuring scores. Videotapes owned by al-Qaeda, seized by US forces in Afghanistan, showed they have experimented with chemical agents using dogs as their victims. In January of 2003, England arrested several terrorists who had the chemical agent ricin in their possession.

Chemical agents fall into five classes: nerve agents, blister agents, blood agents, choking agents, and irritants. The routes of exposure are inhalation, ingestion, and skin absorption/contact. There are too many chemical agents to name here. Most of the chemical agents security professionals worry about are ricin, VX, mustard gas, and various nerve agents like sarin and tabun. Suffice it to say that these agents are easier to obtain and/or manufacture than biological weapons.

Attacks can also include industrial sabotage designed to result in toxic chemical releases, fires, and explosions. In 1984, the accidental release of chemicals from a Union Carbide plant in Bhopal, India killed more than 2,000 people and injured more than 100,000. Clearly, with the heavy concentration of chemical plants in the U.S., terrorists do not have to look to laboratories or third-party providers when they are contemplating a chemical attack.

D. *Nuclear Attacks*

When I was growing up during the days of the Cold War, we had air raid drills in school forcing us to line-up in the hallway and then proceed to the bomb shelter. At some point, I don't remember when, the drills stopped.

Perhaps the drills stopped when the government adopted its new policy of "mutual assured destruction" or MAD. This policy assumed that a nuclear attack from Russia was highly unlikely since our retaliation would surely mean their total destruction as well.

Despite non-proliferation and a host of arms-control treaties, more countries than ever have and continue to develop nuclear weapons. In addition, the widespread adoption of nuclear power as an energy source has created stockpiles of material needed to manufacture nuclear weapons around the world.

According to the State Department, the following countries possess nuclear weapons:

(i) Acknowledged Nuclear Weapons Capability

- Britain
- China

- France
- India
- Pakistan
- Russia
- United States
- North Korea

(ii) Unacknowledged Nuclear Weapons Capability

- Israel

(iii) Seeking Nuclear Weapons Capability

- Iran
- Iraq

The fact that nuclear weapons have gained legitimacy as a "must-have" weapon was evident when India and Pakistan, two countries possessing these weapons, faced off in 2002 and appeared to be ready to engage in another war over the disputed area of Kashmir. Newspapers around the world warned that if these weapons were used, *hundreds of millions* of people would die and the fallout would reach the U.S. and other parts of the world.

Ironically, the end of the Cold War has made the world less secure when it comes to nuclear attack. The break-up of the Soviet Union, the poor state of Russia's economy, and the lack of control and accountability on nuclear material has created a condition where nuclear weapons and the material to make them is easily available.

It was reported within the last 12 months that Chechen rebels, the same group that recently took 700 Russians hostage at a Moscow theatre and who have relationships with radical Arab countries and terror groups, allegedly have stolen weapons-grade plutonium from the new Volgodonskaya nuclear power station near the city of Rostov in Russia.

The precise details of the security breach remain unclear. One US official reported, however, that a significant amount of plutonium was removed together with other radioactive material. Indeed, Russia has an estimated *400 tons* of weapons-grade plutonium considered by western experts to be "at risk" from theft because of poor security. To counter this threat, the U.S. now provides large amounts of money and assistance to Russia to help control the spread of these weapons and materials.

Despite this effort, the National Intelligence Council, an analytical think tank for the 13 agencies that make up the U.S. intelligence community, stated in its annual report to Congress that Russia still represents a serious nuclear proliferation risk and that "weapons-grade and weapons-usable nuclear materials have been stolen from some Russian institutes." In fact, the International Atomic Energy Agency, a Vienna-based division of the United Nations, has documented almost 400 cases of trafficking in nuclear or radiological materials since 1993.

Not surprisingly, al-Qaeda has expressed a clear interest in nuclear know-how and materials to manufacture a crude nuclear or radiological device. Some authors have noted that the Russian KGB has already sold "nuclear suitcases" to al-Qaeda. During the Afghanistan war, bin Laden stated that he already had nuclear weapons and would use them if the U.S. used them first.

"We also believe that bin Laden was seeking to acquire or develop a nuclear device," CIA Director George Tenet told Congress earlier last year. A few months later, in May 2002, the U.S. arrested an alleged al-Qaeda terrorist plotting to build and detonate a dirty bomb in Washington, DC.

What is a "dirty bomb? According to the Council on Foreign Relations, it is a conventional explosive device (not a true nuclear weapon that requires a complex nuclear-fission reaction) that has been packaged with radioactive material, which scatters when the bomb goes off. A dirty bomb kills or injures through the initial blast of the conventional explosive and by airborne radiation and contamination. They are easily manufactured using common materials such as certain cesium isotopes used in cancer treatments, X-ray machines and food preparation machines. While the detonation of such a device may not cause widespread casualties or significant deaths at least initially, the terror and fear it causes would be substantial. The Washington Post reported in March 2002 that the Bush administration's consensus view was that al-Qaeda probably has stolen radioactive contaminants, which could be used to make a dirty bomb.

The nuclear genie is definitely out of the bottle. We can no longer hope and believe that nations or terrorists will act reasonably or responsibly with nuclear devices. It is not possible to be engaged in Détente with terrorists. The nuclear threat to the U.S. is present in various scenarios, which include:

1. Terrorists might try stealing "loose nukes" from the more poorly guarded arsenals of such nuclear powers as Russia or Pakistan.

2. Terrorists might try making crude nuclear weapons from stolen uranium or plutonium.

3. An attack could be launched against a nuclear power plant.

4. An attack could be made against transportation vehicles carrying nuclear spent fuel being delivered to a storage site.

5. A "dirty bomb" could be detonated in a large city.

The al-Qaeda training manual lists nuclear plants as among the best targets for spreading fear in the U.S. According to one top al-Qaeda leader captured in Pakistan, a nuclear power plant in upstate New York was discussed as the initial target for 9/11 but they chose the World Trade Center instead. To confirm the legitimacy of this threat, the federal government has been distributing potassium iodide to people living close to nuclear power plants. This drug, when timely taken, can help prevent thyroid cancer due to radiation exposure.

The death and destruction from a nuclear attack, as well as the psychological and economic damage, are almost too horrible to imagine. And what would the U.S. response be? To whom would its response be directed? While the nuclear attack scenarios may seem unlikely, we need to remember just how unlikely a scenario it was for terrorists to hijack airplanes and fly them into the World Trade Center and the Pentagon. If we fail to take action to prevent these occurrences, we do so at an extremely high risk. Deterrence only works when you have a rational actor. Unfortunately, when it comes to this unconventional war on terrorism that is no longer the case.

Further Thoughts

For the last 30 years or so, Russia and the US could have destroyed most of the planet by unleashing its nuclear weapons. The fact that we have not used these weapons is a remarkable achievement. Deterrence between rational nation states seems to have worked.

In researching this section, it's incredible to me that we are even discussing the use of weapons of mass destruction (WMD). Yet, it is true that these threats exist and the government is making plans to deal with them. The CIA believes that over the next 10 years prospects will grow that more sophisticated weaponry, including WMD indigenously produced or externally acquired—will get into the hands of state and nonstate belligerents that are hostile to the United States. As such, the likelihood will increase over this period that WMD will be used either against the United States or its forces, facilities, and interests overseas.

This is the reality that our children will inherit. I'm really angry about it. Didn't we think about the consequences when we developed these weapons? Did we really believe we could keep them out of the hands of fanatics? How do we get ourselves out of this mess?

As parents we need to do whatever we can to put pressure on our government to work towards finding and destroying these weapons. This is the most important of tasks. We cannot rest on the idea of mutual deterrence anymore…it won't work, as we no longer dealing with rational actors as we have in the past. Just as we would take a gun away from a criminal, we have to do everything in our power to get these weapons under control and out of the hands of madmen and mass murderers. Whatever the cost!

3

Defend Your Homeland

With the threats that now exist in this War on Terror, as responsible parents, what are we supposed to do? The federal government has repeatedly asked us to go about our normal lives but be "vigilant."

Right after the attacks of 9/11, President Bush created the Homeland Security Advisory System (HSAS). It was charged with building a comprehensive communications structure for the dissemination of information regarding the risk of terrorist attacks to all levels of government and the American people. In other words, this is our early warning system for domestic terrorist attacks. The HSAS establishes five threat conditions with associated suggested protective measures:

Low Condition	**Green**	Low risk of terrorist attacks
Guarded Condition	**Blue**	General risk of terrorist attack
Elevated Condition	**Yellow**	Significant risk of terrorist attacks
High Condition	**Orange**	High risk of terrorist attacks
Severe Condition	**Red**	Severe risk of terrorist attacks

A. The TIPS Program

In combination with the alert system, the government announced Operation TIPS, Terrorism Information and Prevention System, to be used to report suspicious and potentially terrorist-related activity. The program was to involve the millions of American workers who, in the daily course of their work, are in a unique position to see unusual or suspicious activity in public places. However, the program has come under heavy assault from civil libertarians and many in Congress.

B. Be Vigilant?

What does "vigilance" mean? In general, you should be "watchful" and "on-guard" for anything suspicious. Don't be fooled into complacency. Don't be paranoid. Exercise *"healthy awareness."* Using your natural born common sense and powers of observation, you should:

- Take notice of odd occurrences or the strange movement of people.

- Take notice of unguarded packages.

- Take notice of abandoned cars or trucks.

- Watch people around crowded and high-risk areas. Are they:

  - Making strange movements.

  - "Casing", "sketching", or "video taping" the area.

  - Communicating on cell phones in a location that would be considered unusual or using walkie-talkies.

  - Notice people who look agitated, nervous, or won't look at you.

- Take notice of events and people around you if you work or are near:

  - Truck and van rentals/leasing

  - Border areas

  - High-profile public events

  - Chemical factories

  - Nuclear power plants or storage areas

  - Airports, bus and train stations

- Water treatment plants and reservoirs
- Refineries
- Crop dusters or plane rental companies
- Government facilities or functions
- Lifelines: Gas, water, electric, sewer lines
- Transportation systems, tunnels, bridges, dams
- Major events with large numbers of people
- Internet or data transmission sites
- Agricultural storage areas

Exercising healthy awareness applies to other situations as well. Al-Qaeda training camps have been discovered in rural Alabama and Oregon. There are "safe-houses" and "sleeper-cells" where the terrorists live in various cities and towns. These can only exist if we do not pay attention to what's happening around us or turn our backs on suspicious activities.

Ask your local police department if they have community anti-terrorism training like CAT Eyes. (See: **http://www. cateyesprogram.com/**). If you observe people or notice something that's not right or see something that's out of place or doesn't belong there, do not attempt to be a hero. Be overly cautious and report it immediately to the police or FBI. If you are traveling and have a cell phone, dial 9-1-1. The operator can connect you to the local police department or other authorities. For the FBI field offices near you, visit **http://www.fbi.gov/contact/fo/info.htm**.

Like most people, I'm sure that you believe that your own vigilance will be meaningless in the broad scope of the war on terrorism. Nothing could be farther from the truth! Imagine the results if we all exercised healthy awareness.

When Mohamed Atta, the ringmaster of 9/11, sought information about crop dusters, the woman who met with him thought he was very odd and suspicious. He became agitated when she did not know who bin Laden was. She did not report the incident to authorities. How do you think she feels now?

Don't close your eyes and ears to things going on around you. On December 22, 2001, thousands of feet above the Atlantic Ocean, passengers on American Airlines Flight 63 saw a commotion and heard cries for help from the flight attendants. They rushed to stop Islamic terrorist Richard Reid from blowing up the airplane. The press reported that as one man reached over the seat to restrain Reid's arms, other passengers secured his legs. They were eventually able to remove Reid's shoe and tie him down using belts and whatever was available. A doctor on board sedated Reid. Another passenger held a fire extinguisher as a weapon while Reid was being restrained. Every passenger on that flight was vigilant and alert. As a result, all 197 people on board made it home safely.

On September 15, 2002, five Arab-American men outside Buffalo were arrested on charges of aiding the al-Qaeda network. Their arrest stemmed from a tip from within the Yemeni community itself in western New York.

Despite the protestations of civil libertarians, we all need to become helpful and additional eyes and ears of the authorities on the lookout for possible terrorist activity. To ignore this obligation or to rely solely on the government is completely impractical. So, exercise healthy awareness, think quickly and be alert, just as the passengers of Flight 63 did. It's up to all of us!

C. Be Prepared to Defend Yourself

We all long for the days when terrorism was something that happened elsewhere. But that is not the world in which we live today. We have to act and think differently if we want to protect ourselves from the latest threat to our family.

In his book, *Secrets of Street Survival—Israeli Style*, self-defense and small-arms expert Eugene Sockut reminds us that creating the correct mindset is as important as anything else when it comes to personal safety and security. Sockut has simple advice in this regard: Always have a game plan because any game plan is better than none at all. Your game plan should take into account weapons and self-defense training. He also reminds us that we need to be on constant alert and not deny or ignore the threats that exist. If you are engaged in a fight, Sockut says, attempt to control the fight, use deadly force if need be, and never give up!

The heroic passengers and crew of Flight 93 that crashed in Pennsylvania on 9/11 understood these instructions all too well. After the plane was hijacked, some passengers phoned loved ones and learned of the World Trade Center and Pentagon incidents. Understanding that they were part of a broader plot against the United States, they announced via cell phone their plan to attack the hijackers who claimed to have a bomb. At a news conference immediately after the crash, U.S. Senator Arlen Specter, R-PA, said that all the facts indicated that a group of passengers and crew rushed the cockpit and brought the plane down before it could be used to attack another U.S. target, most likely the White House or the U.S. Capitol. All 45 passengers and crewmembers on board lost their lives in the disaster. Flight 93 was the only one of the four hijacked planes on 9/11 that did not reach its destination and hit a U.S. landmark.

The heroic spirit of those ordinary men and women demonstrates the nature of the fight against terrorism. In this fight, ordinary citizens may be called upon to do extraordinary things.

Because you never know when YOU will be called on to protect your family or others, you need to be able to defend yourself. For instance:

- Be in good physical shape and condition. (include your kids)

- Take a self-defense course. (include your kids)

- Consider certain weapons (gun, knives, and non-lethal types) and make sure to get proper training and comply with all laws.

- Always have a cell phone and give one to your kids.

The issue of what type of weapon to get is a very personal one. As a parent, I'm fearful of having guns in the house. On the other hand, the bad guys have weapons and if my family is threatened as a result of a major attack, I'm certainly going to want to protect them with whatever is at my disposal. Is this farfetched? Who knows? The fact remains that having the right weapon can prevent harm to you and your family. To review other types of weapons and self-defense products currently available see: **http://www.pimall.com/nais/e.menu-e.html** or **http://www.allamericanprotection.com**

You can't ignore the threats that exist to your family's personal safety. Being vigilant and physically prepared will make you feel less vulnerable and in control of your destiny. You never know when you may need to defend yourself in a life-threatening situation.

Further Thoughts

As Americans, we inherently distrust government. We cherish our freedom and our privacy. But in this unconventional war we all have to become an extension to the government, an extra set of eyes and ears. While preventing another attack is a huge task, we all have to be involved.

The 9/11 attacks prompted new laws and ideas that are threatening to alter the landscape in the name of national security. Laws like the US Patriot Act and the new Department of Homeland Security clearly show that things are changing…and rapidly. Whether we like it or not, our privacy and freedom are being threatened.

Racial profiling of Middle Eastern men was unthinkable before 9/11. Keeping people incarcerated or conducting a trial without access to an attorney was also difficult to imagine. There is a lesson to be learned. We need to be flexible when our national and personal security is at risk. Our ideals of freedom can be compromised quickly when faced with grave harm to our security. They should not be lost or changed without a great deal of thought and concern. This is a challenge for all of us.

Like the TIPS Program, the issues of privacy versus security are being hotly debated and will likely to continue for years. Personally, I'm not sure where I stand on them. On one hand, I know that the government can do immense harm to individual rights if not properly checked. On the other hand, I feel that our government needs ammunition to fight terrorism. If you are not doing anything wrong, it stands to reason, you should have nothing to hide. And I get incredibly angry when our enemies use our freedoms of speech and our judicial system to organize and propagandize against us.

Whichever way it turns out, I hope that for our sake we strike a correct balance. If not, our enemies win.

4

A Call To Action

CITIZEN ACTIVISM

Whether or not you agree with some of the political issues outlined in Chapter 1, there are things you can do to influence public and foreign policy and affect positive change. The connection between political involvement and change is clear to all of those who protested during the Vietnam War. Those protests changed the outcome and direction of the war.

A. *Vote*

In 1996, only 49% of the U.S. registered voters cast a ballot for President. This was the lowest turn out since 1924. The election result of 2000 between Al Gore and George W. Bush in terms of voter participation was only about 50%. And the ultimate decision in that election came down to a few thousand votes in Florida. If you want to make an impact and make sure your voice is heard, exercise your right to vote!

I often think about how bizarre the 2000 Presidential race was. A few ballots (in Florida), along with the US Supreme Court, effectively put Bush into office despite the fact he failed to win the popular vote. I didn't vote for Bush and I'm not happy about some of his domestic programs, but his strong response to 9/11 has convinced me that he is the right man, and has the right team, for the job with respect to fighting this war.

B. *Become Active with a Political Action Committee or Interest Group*

Political Action Committees or PACs are organizations established by private groups to support candidates for public office or a group cause. Interest groups are similar. By acting collectively towards a common goal and combining financial and political forces, your chances of affecting change are increased exponentially. There are too many to mention, but here are some organizations that fight hate and promote better understanding and dialogue:

1. *Southern Poverty Law Center*

   http://www.SPLCenter.org

2. *Anti-Defamation League*

   http://www.adl.org

3. *American Arab Anti-Discrimination Committee*

   http://www.adc.org

4. *Council on American-Islamic Relations*

   http://www.cair-net.org

5. *National Conference for Community Justice*

   http://www.nccj.org

6. *Citizens Making a Difference*

   http://www.moveon.org/

7. *Black America's Political Action Committee*

   http://www.bampac.org/

8. *Protect Our Heritage*

   <u>http://www.protectourheritagepac.org/default.asp</u>

C. *Contact your Elected Officials*

Write to elected officials and tell them how you feel about certain policies and other matters relating to policy in our battle against terrorism. Don't assume they don't care. They do listen. They have to in order to get re-elected. E-mail is an easy method. For a listing of the e-mail address to your Congressional leaders go to **http://www. geocities.com/CapitolHill/1411/index.html**. To e-mail President Bush and other federal officials visit **http://www. emailthepresident.com**. You might be surprised, they may even respond back to you!

D. *Work for the Federal Government or Enlist in the Armed Forces*

For a good start, see **http://www.usajobs.opm.gov/**. For military positions see **http://www.armedforcescareers.com/**

E. *Volunteer Your Time*

The 9/11 attacks have brought out a spirit of community and volunteerism. Thanks to President Bush, people are more committed than ever to help each other. In his January 29, 2002, State of the Union address, the President asked that Americans volunteer their services to improve and safeguard our country. At that time he announced the new USA Freedom Corps which focuses on three areas of need: responding in case of crisis at home, rebuilding our communities, and extending American compassion throughout the world. "We want to be a Nation that serves goals larger than self. We have been offered a unique opportunity, and we must not let this moment pass." Get your children involved early so that they understand their responsibility to our community. See the following web sites for further volunteer information:

- Peace Corps: **http://www.peacecorps.gov/indexf.cfm**

- Citizen Corps: **http://www.citizencorps.gov/**

- AmeriCorps: **http://www.americorps.gov/**

- Senior Corps: **http://www.seniorcorps.org/**

- U.S.A. Freedom Corps: **http://usafreedomcorps.gov/**

- Points of Light Foundation: **http://www.pointsoflight.org/**

- Neighborhood Watch Program: **http://www.usaonwatch.org/**

- National Guard: **http://www.ngb.dtic.mil/**

- CERT Program: **http://training.fema.gov/EMIWeb/cert/**

- Volunteer for your town fire, medic and first responder groups

Teach your children about the memorable words of the late President John F. Kennedy, *"Ask not, what your country can do for you; ask, what you can do for your country."*

F. *Put Your Money Where Your Mouth Is!*

1. *Citizen Sanctions*

Your pocketbook can speak a lot in this war on terror. The experts will tell you that economic sanctions against countries don't always work. This is especially true if we are the only country using them. But sanctions should be part of our citizen strategy when dealing with countries that sponsor terror, as well as against other nations that continue to support those regimes.

Even if the government doesn't support economic sanctions against these states, we, as citizens, do not have to travel, support or purchase products originating from these countries. The countries include Iraq, Iran, Syria, Egypt, Saudi Arabia, Libya, Pakistan and Sudan. While you probably haven't purchased a TV or DVD from any of these countries lately, our refusal to help finance secondary states like <u>France, China and Russia</u> should be on our prohibited list as well. These countries give continued support to those radical Arab regimes. They are the main exporters of weapons and nuclear technology to those states. Why finance their economies, which in the end ultimately helps our enemies? So buy American, <u>check the labels when you shop</u>, particularly in specialty stores where products from these countries may be available and make a stand with your pocketbook!

2. Charitable Donations

Your charitable donations, either in cash or other property, can go a long way in promoting tolerance and human rights. You might even get a tax break. There are obviously too many charities to mention, but some include:

- The American Red Cross

    http://www.redcross.org/

- America's Fund for Afghan Children, c/o The White House, 1600 Pennsylvania Avenue, Washington, DC 20509-1600

- American Liberty Partnership, a coordinated effort for many charities **http://www.libertyunites.org/donate.adp**

- Families of Freedom Scholarship Fund

    http://www.familiesoffreedom.org/

- WTC Relief Home Page

  http://www.wtcrelief.info/Charities/Information/pages/Home.jsp

- United Way

  http://national.unitedway.org/

- Save One Person

  http://saveoneperson.org/

- Save The Children

  http://www.savethechildren.org/

3. *Investments With A Conscience*

If you're like me, your totally depressed with the status of your investments and 401k in light of the stock market crash. I can't view my year-end statements without feeling ill. Even my children's college fund savings is in the toilet.

You may want to consider investment ideas that promote various social causes:

- Purchase Series EE Patriot Bonds, U.S. Savings Bonds, and Treasury Bills to express your support for our nation's war and recovery efforts.

- Donate tax refunds and gifts to the U.S. government (See: **http://www.fms.treas.gov/news/factsheets/gifts.html**)

- Invest in start-up companies specializing in

  - Clean renewable energy products

  - Security-enhancement products

  - Biotech companies researching new vaccines

- Invest in Socially Responsible Mutual Funds. Some examples include:

  - Calvert Group—offers investors a large family of socially responsible equity, bond, and money-market funds.

  - Domini Social Investments—manages assets for individual and institutional investors who wish to integrate social and environmental criteria into their investment decisions.

  - Enterprise Global Socially Responsive Fund—growth-oriented mutual fund which gives investors the opportunity to merge their personal values with their financial objectives.

  - Green Century Funds—founded by non-profit environmental organizations in 1991, these are a family of no-load environmentally responsible mutual funds.

  - New Alternatives Fund—socially responsible fund with investments in renewable energy, fuel cells, recycling and energy conservation, and organic foods.

  - Parnassus Investments—the mutual fund company that does well by doing good.

  - SocialFunds.com—resource for information on socially responsible mutual funds.

  - Web Directory—Socially and/or Environmentally Screened Funds

G. Get Creative

CNN reported that Jon Messner, a self-proclaimed Web warrior who runs an Internet porn site, enlisted in the war on terror by hacking into an Internet site run by al-Qaeda. Messner said he "hijacked" al Neda for five days and recorded a "virtual who's-who of every hostile message board and site on the Internet." Traffic to the site increased under his control, most of it coming from Saudi Arabia, he said. If Jon Messner can come up with an idea, be creative and come up with one yourself! We all have a part to play.

Final Thoughts

I refuse to believe that I am powerless to have an impact on this war. The idea that through involvement I can affect the outcome of this war, however small that may be, and not be a passive actor has been extremely comforting. I discovered there are things I can do. Part of coping with our new reality is getting involved and being engaged on some level. And just image what would happen if we all moved collectively in the same direction and with the same purpose. We could move mountains.

5

Give Me Shelter

While prevention and vigilance are the keys to avoiding future attacks, equally as important is your own disaster recovery plan in the event an attack should occur.

Every major business in the country has a disaster recovery plan. It outlines what they will do if the unthinkable happens…a fire, a flood, an earthquake, a hurricane, and, of course in this era, a terrorist attack. Once a year or even more often, business leaders test and update these plans.

Proper planning can help to deal with attacks. Developing a disaster plan involves putting together material and procedures to resume normal life during and following a disaster, making sure your family is aware of what they need to do in an emergency, and making revisions to the plan as necessary. With a viable plan you can recover with minimal chaos and save lives.

Right after the second plane struck the World Trade Towers, I obviously knew we were under attack. Since I live and work near New York, I wanted to speak to my wife and make sure she and the children were ok. I was unable to reach her as the phones were overloaded. I finally reached her on her cell phone and told her to get our son out of school and meet me at her mom's house. For the first time in my life, I saw firsthand how important it is to have a plan of communication and readiness. If you don't have one, you should review in detail the Family Disaster Plan and Supply Checklist in Appendix I at the end of this book for ideas on having such a plan.

There are a host of books coming out on how to prepare for an attack. Some of these scare the hell out of me. They describe a society breaking down after an attack where we will need to have a shelter to live in for months. While I do not go that far in describing a rational disaster recovery plan, you may want to review some of these materials, as they do provide some valuable information. {See: **http://www. survivingterrorism.com** or *A Citizen's Guide to Terrorism Preparedness* by Armando Bevelacqua and Richard Stilp.

Whatever your level of preparedness, at the very least, you should have basic plan which includes disaster supplies. Having a plan and understanding how it works can be two different things. Your family needs to be completely aware of the plan. Once a year, re-check your supplies and teach your children where the supplies are. Do they know how to turn on the flashlights? Do they know what to do if you're out of town? Do they know which room is your own 'safe room' when a disaster occurs? The time to teach them is not when the problem occurs.

REASONABLE RESPONSES TO THE THREATS THAT EXIST

I want to take a moment and discuss some very basic ideas to deal with the threats mentioned in Chapter 2. In the event of an attack, first and foremost, follow the disaster plans and materials found in Appendix I. Secondly, don't panic. Remember your children are relying on you to take control of the situation. Hopefully, some of the information here will help.

A. Biological Responses and Treatment

In his book, *When Every Moment Counts*, U.S. Senator and physician Bill Frist gives practical solutions to dealing with the bio-terrorism threat. These plans are meant to confront the fear as much as the bioterror weapon itself. He believes that knowledge and preparation are the keys to attacking this fear head-on.

The U.S. government is responding to the threat of bioterrorism by increasing funding for research, public health initiatives, vaccine and drug stockpiles, hospital preparedness, and disease surveillance and response systems at the federal, state, and local levels.

However, when I speak to my local police and fire chief, they tell me that they still do not have enough money or the proper information, surveillance and equipment to deal with a major terrorist attack. Further, they tell me that coordination between the states and federal government is not very good and that they learn more from CNN than they do from the federal authorities.

In 2002, the Council of Foreign Relations sponsored an independent Task Force to examine the country's preparedness to deal with terrorism. One year after 9/11, the Task Force, chaired by ex-US Senators Gary Hart and Warren Rudman, found "America remains dangerously unprepared to prevent and respond to a catastrophic terrorist attack on U.S. soil." To review the full report see: **http://www.cfr.org/publication.php?id=5099**. Undoubtedly, a *lot* still needs to be done.

Much of the following material on biological responses was taken from the CDC, which is recognized as the lead federal agency for protecting the health and safety of American citizens. Access the CDC website at **http://www.cdc.gov**. Other information can be obtained at *www.bt.cdc.gov*.

1. Anthrax Prevention and Treatment

(i) <u>Vaccines</u>. There is an anthrax vaccine, and more effective ones are being developed. The current vaccine is reported to be 93% effective in protecting against anthrax. Only high-risk individuals should be vaccinated.

(ii) <u>Antibiotics</u>. For treatment, antibiotics are effective if initiated early. If left untreated, the disease can be fatal. The Food and Drug Administration (FDA) has approved a limited number of products for the treatment of anthrax including Ciprofloxacin (Cipro), doxycycline, and penicillin G procaine. But note that the Federal Trade Commission (FTC) has warned citizens not to purchase these drugs over the Internet. Speak to a doctor or health professional before taking these drugs, as there are side effects. While the government and physicians suggest you not purchase Cipro or other drugs over the Internet, they are easily available {See: **http://www.mexico-canada-prescriptions-drugs-online-mexican-pharmacy.com/index.htm**}. Again, as with many of the issues outlined in this book, these are very personal questions that you should thoroughly investigate and then make an informed decision.

(iii) <u>Be wary of the mail</u>. In light of the recent anthrax attacks, the U.S. Postal Service advises that individuals be suspicious of letters or packages with any powdery substance on them, regardless of color.

Teach your children about the following directions:

Identifying Suspicious Packages and Envelopes

Some characteristics of suspicious packages and envelopes include the following:

- Inappropriate or unusual labeling
- Excessive postage
- Handwritten or poorly typed addresses
- Misspellings of common words
- Strange return address or no return address
- Incorrect titles or title without a name
- Not addressed to a specific person
- Marked with restrictions, such as "Personal," "Confidential," or "do not x-ray"
- Marked with any threatening language

- Postmarked from a city or state that does not match the return address

Powdery substance felt through or appearing on the package or envelope

- Oily stains, discolorations, or odor
- Lopsided or uneven envelope
- Excessive packaging material such as masking tape, string, etc.

Other suspicious signs

- Excessive weight
- Protruding wires or aluminum foil

If a package or envelope appears suspicious, do not open or shake it. Call the police or FBI.

2. Smallpox Prevention and Treatment

(i) <u>Vaccines</u>: In the U.S., routine vaccination against smallpox ended in 1972. While the vaccine is not readily available, President Bush is considering new and widespread vaccination programs. He has already ordered that military and first responder personnel get vaccinated. To prove its safe, he was also vaccinated. The CDC believes that approximately half of the U.S. population has never been vaccinated. The level of immunity, if any, among persons who were vaccinated before 1972 is uncertain; therefore, these persons are assumed to be susceptible. This means that nearly the entire U.S. population has partial immunity at best. Immunity can be boosted effectively with a single revaccination. Prior infection with the disease grants lifelong immunity.

There can be severe side effects to the smallpox vaccine, which is why the President's decision on mass vaccinations is a difficult one. In the event of a smallpox outbreak, the CDC has clear guidelines to swiftly provide vaccine to people exposed to the disease. In order to make certain that the country has enough vaccine on hand; President Bush has requested additional funds to speed the development and acquisition of more smallpox vaccine. If administered within a few days of exposure to the virus, the smallpox vaccine is not only the best protection, but also the only known cure for the disease.

(ii) Treatment. Other than the vaccine, there is no proven treatment for smallpox. Research to evaluate new antiviral agents is, however, ongoing. Patients with smallpox can benefit from supportive therapy (e.g., intravenous fluids, medicine to control fever or pain) and antibiotics for any secondary bacterial infections that may occur as the result of the viral infection. Because it is a virus, antibiotics such as Ciprofloxacin will not fight smallpox.

In the event of outbreak, take following steps:

- Quarantine: Patients should be placed in medical isolation so that they will not continue to spread the virus. In addition, people who have come into close contact with smallpox patients should be vaccinated immediately and closely watched for symptoms of smallpox. Vaccination and isolation are the main strategies for stopping the spread of smallpox.

- Contamination: Contaminated clothing or bed linen can also spread the virus so special precautions need to be taken to ensure that all bedding and clothing of patients are cleaned appropriately with bleach and hot water. Disinfectants such as bleach and quaternary ammonia can be used for cleaning contaminated surfaces. You should remove and correctly dispose of all protective clothing before contact with non-vaccinated people.

I don't know about you but the recurring pictures of people scarred with smallpox shown in the newspapers are scarring the hell out of me. The issue of whether you should get vaccinated (should it become available) is a difficult one. The risk has to be weighed against the possibility of an attack versus the side effects associated with the vaccine. We were supposed to be rid of the deadly disease, but once again it has reared its ugly head as a potential bio-weapon. I urge you to read and speak to as many health professionals as you can before making any decisions on this difficult subject. A good place to start on the vaccination issue, which has excellent links is: **http://www.nlm.nih. gov/medlineplus/smallpox.html#alternativetherapy**. For various alternative treatments see: **http://www.chetday. com/smallpoxepidemic.htm**.

B. Chemical Attack Prevention and Treatment

If you believe you have been exposed to a chemical agent, you need to take steps to protect and decontaminate yourself immediately. Take the following actions:

1. Evacuate the Area: Avoid or flee the contaminated area, shielding your eyes and skin as much as possible, and minimizing the amount inhaled. Find sealed rooms or areas on higher floors that are closed off to ventilation (basements are not suggested for chemical attacks). You can seal a room by using duct tape around the door jam.

2. Clothing. Remove all your clothing, jewelry, glasses, wigs, etc. and limit the amount of time the agent is in contact with skin.

3. Wash Down. Water alone is a universal way to decontaminate yourself. Use talcum powder or flour if water is not available. Use soap if you have it, but do not delay decontamination. Blot clean and dry with an absorbent cloth.

4. Gas Masks: Currently, the CDC does not recommend consumers purchase any particular product, including gas masks, to protect against biological or chemical attacks. However, facemasks should be used. Bill Frist in *When Every Moment Counts*, suggests a simple mask with a filter manufactured by 3M with a rating of N95. These are available at most hardware and home supply stores.

In summary, the primary goal with respect to biological and chemical attacks is:

1. Leave the area

2. Limit exposure

3. Protect your breathing airways as much as possible; use a wet cloth to prevent inhalation

4. Take steps to decontaminate yourself as quickly as possible

5. Follow the shelter in place guidelines described in "C" below. (But search out higher floors for biological or chemical attacks)

Further Information Sources

Further information on bioterrorism and public health preparedness from the CDC again at **http://www.bt.cdc.gov/**. For more information about the specific effects of chemical or biological agents, the following Web sites may be helpful:

- U.S. Department of Energy: **http://energy.gov/**

- Southern Illinois University: **http://www.lib.siu.edu/hp/websites/bioterrorism.shtml**

- The University of Minnesota Center for Infectious Disease Research and Policy: **http://www1.umn.edu/cidrap/content/bt/bioprep/**

- U.S. Department of Health and Human Services: **http://www.hhs.gov/**

- Federal Emergency Management Agency: **http://www.rris.fema.gov/**

- Environmental Protection Agency: **http://www.epa.gov/swercepp/cntr-ter.html**

- The National Response Team: **http://www.nrt.org/**

- Center for Civilian Bio-defense Strategies: **http://www.hopkins-biodefense.org**

C. Nuclear Preparedness and Treatment

Planning and Preparing Your Shelter

In the event of a nuclear type attack, you should:

- Evacuate immediately to shelters, subways, basements, etc. Taking shelter could reduce exposure to gamma radiation.

- To be effective, such shelters would need:

  - Sealed doors and windows, as well as sanitation, air circulation, and filtration equipment.

  - They should also contain food, water, and medical supplies.

  - If feasible, pick a room with a toilet, water, and phone (wireless and cell phone would probably work).

  - Large enough for family or co-workers.

  - Have a shelter-in-place kit that has pre-cut and labeled plastic sheeting for windows, doors, and vents. Be sure to cut plastic large enough to completely cover the area.

  - Lock all doors and windows for a better seal and close all vents and fireplace dampers.

  - Turn off heating/air conditioning systems.

  - Have Disaster Supplies Kit ready—especially water, battery-powered radio, extra batteries, and flashlight. *See: Disaster Planning Supply List in Appendix I.

  - Have snacks and books to make the situation more comfortable.

- If you are exposed to fallout you could reduce the contamination by breathing through a wet cloth, removing contaminated clothing, and showering as soon as possible after exposure to slough off radioactive dust.

- You should postpone entering contaminated areas to allow radiation levels to decrease naturally; for example, by waiting 3–7 days after the explosion before entering a contaminated area.

- Don't leave a shelter area in your home or in a public place until told to do so.

- <u>Potassium Iodide</u>: Children, pregnant women, and nursing mothers should take potassium iodide immediately to prevent the destruction of the thyroid or potential development of thyroid cancer. (Potassium iodide provides no protection against other types of radiation damage, for which there is no known protective agent.) Review the FDA recommendations on potassium iodide on the Web at: **http://www.fda.gov/cder/guidance/5052fnl.htm**.

  - To obtain Potassium Iodide go to:

    - **http://www.nukepills.com/pages/749857/index.htm**;

    - **http://www.anbex.com/**; or

    - **http://readyprep.com/Merchant2/merchant.mv?Screen=CTGY&Store_Code=R&Category_Code=RB**

More Information on Nuclear Preparedness

To find more information about radiation health effects, emergency response and related matters in the event of a nuclear attack, see:

- The Nuclear Regulatory Commission: **http://www.nrc.gov/**

- Nuclear War Survival Skills at **http://www.oism.org/nwss**

- The Environmental Protection Agency: **http://www.epa.gov/**

- Emergency Response Program can be reached at (301) 415-8200.

- The Federal Emergency Management Agency (FEMA) **http://www.fema.gov/**

- The Radiation Emergency Assistance Center/Training Site (REAC/TS) can be reached at (865)-576-3131.

Further Thoughts

There are many resources and information available on these matters. I have listed numerous helpful sites in Appendix II. Books are coming out every day about how to prepare for the worse case scenario. There is also any number of "experts" whose advice may include doing nothing or, in the extreme, buying a complete chemical warfare suit and building a shelter you can live in for months. Remember immediately after the attacks of 9/11, it was virtually impossible to find any kind of mask available in any store in the United States.

It's unlikely that you will find yourself right in the middle of an attack. But we all need to know that the wind carrying chemical or biological agents or nuclear fallout may pose the real danger.

Regardless of what you think about the possibility of these types of attacks, for the sake of your children it makes sense to be prepared. What's the harm? People that live in California plan for earthquakes. People in the tornado belt plan for these natural disasters as well. Besides, a sense of control over these issues is the best remedy for stress. I suspect you have disability or life insurance. Well shouldn't you also have disaster planning and supplies as well? It starts with planning and preparing for the worst. Hopefully the worst will never happen.

6

Helping Children Cope with the Threat of Terrorism

The threat of terrorism instills as much fear and anxiety as the act of violence itself. In early November 2002, we learned through a released audiotape that bin Laden was still alive. During the same time, the FBI released a warning that they were picking up "chatter" that al-Qaeda was preparing for "spectacular attacks to disrupt the U.S. economy and inflict massive casualties". These statements continually instill fear and anxiety in all of us…especially our children.

My own feelings of helplessness in protecting my children are the very reasons I began writing this book in July 2002. I knew in my heart that I had to do something. Doing nothing was not an option. But no matter how prepared we may be, the question remains, how do we go about our lives in a productive manner and plan for the future when our society is under the constant threat of serious harm? How do help our children cope with the constant feelings of fear and insecurity?

As a parent, I have managed to deal with these matters by taking the following steps:

1. Obtain as much knowledge about the situation as possible.

2. Don't rely on the government to protect you.

3. Be prepared for all contingencies…without being paranoid.

4. Try to live life and cherish each day as much as possible.

5. Pray and have faith that everything will turn out all right.

A. *Obtain As Much knowledge About The Situation As Possible.*

If you believe that knowledge is power, then you have to take responsibility for learning about the potential threats to your family and the things you can do to prevent these threats. This book was intended to give you some ideas to address these very issues. History gives us plenty of examples where people's failure to understand the severity of a situation led to disaster. It always puzzled me why the Jews in 1930 Germany didn't take the Nazis more seriously until it was too late? Understanding the risks to you and your family will help you decide what actions you need to take to protect them.

In addition, we need to teach our children that our enemy is just a handful of radical Islamic fundamentalists, and not the millions of peaceful Muslims living among us. We need to diffuse the fear or hatred of strangers or foreigners. That is not, in our diverse country, an option. Only through knowledge (and wisdom) can we have the correct response to this conflict.

Charles Kettering said that you should give a lot of thought to the future because that is where you are going to spend the rest of your life. One of the greatest mistakes that people can make, and the one with the worst long-term consequences, is to think only about the present and give very little thought to what might happen in the months and years ahead.

B. *It's Impractical To Completely Rely On The Government.*

Congress has just approved the Homeland Security bill. This new department, created to protect the homeland, will create a 170,000-employee department dedicated to fighting terrorism and protecting our country. It will create a Cabinet-level department out of all or parts of 22 agencies including Customs, INS and the Transportation Security Administration with a $37 billion budget.

However, the new department doesn't address the really important elements of making us safer. It doesn't strengthen the Federal Emergency Management Administration (FEMA), doesn't include the two most important agencies (FBI and CIA), and it doesn't create better information sharing with local police. I'm not sure I feel any safer because we have a bigger federal bureaucracy.

But as I said previously, it is completely impractical to believe that the government can fully protect us in a country so large and open as ours. That's why we all have to exercise "healthy awareness" to help the government and each other in any way we can. To rely on the government to be able to handle all these matters, and protect us completely, is not only impractical, as a parent it's outright negligent.

Taking the steps outlined in this book will not only make you more prepared, it will undoubtedly make you feel more empowered. The helplessness and anxiety I felt before I began this journey has abated due to the actions I have taken. I am now more knowledgeable, better prepared, and more capable of dealing with and surviving an attack…and so are my children. As a result, I am better able to cope with all the warnings and uncertainty that exists.

C. Be As Prepared As Possible For All Contingencies…Without Being Paranoid.

Each of us has to decide for ourselves what level, if any, of preparedness we will exercise. Prior to 9/11, I never prepared for any type disaster; whether it was Y2K or any other prophesy of doom. But since 9/11, I have a small amount of Cipro in my house; enough food and water for 5 days, and a disaster plan to tell my family what to do in the event of a major attack. These difficult questions have no easy answers. It all depends on your own personal level of concern.

At first, I felt incredibly sad and angry when I went to the store to purchase my Disaster Supplies. (*See Appendix I for a complete list of needed supplies*) But I felt that it would be completely irresponsible for me not to be prepared. I had to **DO SOMETHING**. These negative emotions I experienced purchasing my Disaster Supplies soon turned into feelings of empowerment knowing that if the stores can't get water or food due to a disruption of some sort, I won't have to look at my children and see them hungry or thirsty because I did not take these threats seriously. By doing nothing, I felt vulnerable and dependent. By taking action, I felt more in control and independent...and better able to cope.

D. Live Life To The Fullest

This is such an overused statement. Yet how many of us really take it seriously? I work too hard and spent too little time with my family. I'm overly concerned about money, my job and other things to the point of unnecessary worry and stress. What a waste!

If you find that you need help with certain issues, or just dealing with everyday stress and anxiety, try these following exercises:

1. Exercise & Stretch (move your body as much as you can)

2. Eat well...take care of yourself

3. Breath deeply and evenly (blow out stressful hot air)

4. Work pleasures into your day

5. Laugh as much as you can

6. Play as much as you can

7. Do what makes you happy...find your passion and purpose!

8. Avoid crutches (I started smoking after 9/11...but have since quit...again!)

9. Cry

10. Mediate/Yoga

11. Listen to soothing music

12. Scream

Whether you know someone directly affected by 9/11 or not, you can still suffer from substantial psychological stress due to this new threat. This is sometimes referred to as "secondary post-traumatic stress disorder". You may be feeling anxious, having trouble sleeping, afraid of flying, going into a city, or even leaving the house. You may be having problems concentrating, marital problems or many other type symptoms.

American Physchological Association members and experts Rona M. Fields, Ph.D., and Joe Margolin, Ph.D., suggest the following with respect to coping with terrorism:

1. Identify the feelings that you may be experiencing. Understand that your feelings are a normal reaction to an abnormal situation.

2. Remember that you have overcome adversity and trauma in the past. Try to remember what you did that helped you overcome the fear and helplessness in that situation.

3. Talk to others about your fears. It's okay to ask for help. Workplaces may convene small groups with a mental health counselor so people can share feelings.

4. Make efforts to maintain your usual routine.

5. Think positively. Realize that things will get better. Be realistic about the time it takes to feel better.

6. Recognize that the nature of terrorist attacks creates fear and uncertainty about the future. Continue to do the things in your life that you enjoy. Don't get preoccupied with the things you cannot control to the extent that they prevent you from living your normal life.

7. Know the actions our government is taking action to combat terrorism and restore safety and security. Recognize that trained officials throughout the country are mobilized to prevent, prepare for and respond to terrorist attacks.

8. Limit exposure to media coverage.

Tips For Helping Your Children Cope

In a poll of 2500 children taken by Public Broadcasting, 50% of more than said they think about 9/11 once a week or more and 19% said they think about it every day. The Connecticut Commission on Children in writing a report titled "Children in the Wake of Terrorism, One Year Later" (which can be found on the Web at **http:// www.cga.state.ct.us/coc/oneyearlaterupdated.htm**) discovered that children have real concerns about the events of 9/11, which included the need to feel safe at home and school, the need to have heroes (police and firemen) and a connection to the community.

"9/11 will remain the major backdrop for their growing years, just as World War II and the Cold War influenced their parents and grandparents."

To help your children deal with the stress of terrorism:

1. Encourage your children to say how they are feeling about the event.

2. Ask them what they have seen, heard or experienced.

3. Don't promise your children that nothing bad will happen but assure them that you are taking care of them, will protect them and will continue to help them deal with anything that makes them feel afraid.

4. Help them recognize when they have shown courage in meeting a new scary situation and accomplished a goal despite hardship or barriers. Instill a sense of empowerment.

5. Let them know that institutions are still in place and our government is intact.

6. Know that it is possible for children to experience vicariously the traumatization from the terrorist attack (e.g. watching TV coverage, overhearing adult conversations).

7. Spend more time with your children and let them be more dependent on you during the months following the trauma—for example, allowing your child to cling to you more often than usual. Physical affection is very comforting to children who have experienced trauma.

8. Provide play experiences to help relieve tension. Younger children in particular may find it easier to share their ideas and feelings about the event through non-verbal activities such as drawing.

9. Encourage your older children to speak with you, and with one another, about their thoughts and feelings. This helps reduce their confusion and anxiety related to the trauma. Respond to questions in terms they can comprehend. Reassure them repeatedly that you care about them and that you understand their fears and concerns.

10. Love them, spend time with them, listen and comfort them.

11. Above all, the better you learn to manage your own feelings, the better your children will cope

The American Psychological Association has a lot of helpful information:

- 'Talk to Someone Who Can Help' brochure about psychotherapy and choosing a psychologist from the American Psychological Association can be ordered free of charge. Call 1-800-964-2000

- Get the facts: How to find help through psychotherapy, a brief question-and-answer guide that provides basic information about psychotherapy and how it can help. **www.helping.apa.org/therapy/psychotherapy.html**

- Find a Psychologist, information on how to be connected with the state psychological association referral network in your area. This information is also available by calling: 1-800-964-2000. **www.helping.apa.org/find.html**

See Appendix II for more material on this important topic.

Our enemies win if they succeed in making us so fearful or anxious that we alter our lifestyle or way of life. Part of their envy and hatred of us is our eternal optimism and view of life. So more than ever, we need to make conscious decisions to savor each and every day. Whatever that means in your world…take steps to make it your reality.

E. Lord, Help Us in This Battle

I am not a very religious person. While I believe in God, I am not sure whether organized religion offers the correct outlet for my spiritual expression. Personally, I deplore the killing, wars and corruption that have been perpetuated in the name of religion. The War on Terrorism is one such example. Recently, certain Christian Right leaders have come out and said very distasteful things about Islam and Mohammed. All over the world Muslims are fighting Christians, Jews, Hindus, and Buddhists, and well…you know the rest. Everyone seems to believe they speak for God. It's enough to make you want to become an atheist.

Right after 9/11, pastors and preachers began fielding questions from people as to whether this was the end of days as reported in the book of Revelation. The Left Behind series by Tim LaHaye and Jerry Jenkins, based on the events foretold in the book of Revelation, have become best sellers, as many Christians believe Christ is coming again in an ultimate battle with the Anti-Christ. For some people, 9/11 was a sign of this apocalyptic event.

I was driving in my car the other day and scanned over to a radio station that was playing gospel; not something I usually listen to. The song playing was by Yolanda Adams and was about "the battle was not yours but the Lords." It was an interesting and calming moment for me.

While we all have a part to play, in the end what will be…will be. God has a plan, always has. By prayer and faith, we can and will find peace in that message alone. As throughout human history God's plan has always been the right one.

Conclusion

It is now January 22, 2003. More than a year has passed since I stood in stunned silence and watched the smoke rising from the World Trade Center and the Pentagon.

Four short months ago, September 11, 2002, the anniversary of the attack, our nation went on "high alert." Vice-President Dick Cheney was moved to an undisclosed secure location. Anti-aircraft batteries were guarding various Washington sites. The country was reliving the horrors of 9/11 and experiencing the changes it brought.

9/11 had an incredible impact on the nation's landscape and our national psyche. As a result of neglect or indifference, the Islamic fundamentalist virus had turned into a plague, and like any deadly disease, it will continue to stalked us until its destroyed and eradicated. All at once, we lost our innocence and everything changed. Once again, we cursed ourselves for not taking this threat more seriously, for being lulled into complacency, for not being prepared.

With trillions of retirement money lost, rising layoffs, and just everyday issues of work, family and raising children, it's easy to forget **WE ARE AT WAR.** We are at war around the world, and at home. But we must never forget our armed forces protecting us, our police and firemen who are the first line of response, the people who died on 9/11, or the brave and heroic passengers and crew of Flight 93. If our immediate sorrow turned to anger, it's time now for it to turn to defiance and resolve that the next time this happens, we will be better prepared.

In the aftermath of the tragic events that have taken place, we have to understand that we are a strong people who have and will continue to come together to make certain that we prevail in this struggle. General Douglas McArthur once said: "There is no security in this world, only opportunity." Take this opportunity to make a difference, not just in the fight against terrorism, but in the important responsibility you have as a parent to teach your children to respect others and be tolerate of their differences. It is our children who will inherent the results of the decisions we make, and the actions we take, in this unconventional war.

While this book recommends taking certain steps to prevent and prepare for a terrorist attack, it's important to remember to have faith, be calm, and make sure you enjoy each day of your life. That sounds strange to those of us living under the constant reminder of a Yellow alert from the Homeland Security Agency, but it is exactly what our parents, grandparents and great-grandparents did during World War II. Even with the threat of German U-Boats appearing off the coast of New Jersey where I now vacation with my wife and children, they went on living their lives. They were supportive of the troops abroad and they were vigilant. They conserved resources. They reported suspicious people and activity. They became as much of a weapon as any plane or tank or ship.

In the same way, living a full and rewarding life is the best thing you can do to deal with the insecurity and insanity that exists today. Use this time in your life to find your passion and purpose. Take time to smell the roses, laugh each day, hug your kids, and help as many people you can. In all areas of your life, speak to the senselessness of violence, hate, intolerance, and prejudice. Limit your television, radio and Internet activity in order to avoid excessive exposure to imagery of the death, damage, and destruction. Despite these threats, we are resilient and will survive. This too shall pass.

Engage in prayer. God needs to hear from you. In praying, you will gain strength and solace in these difficult times. It is also a time to pray for all of those families who have been touched by the destruction and loss of life in this war. The power of collective prayer is just what we need to regain the sanity for a peaceful future.

Be hopeful, as there are positive signs of change. Internationally, the Russians are reconsidering their nuclear deal with Iran. Afghanistan no longer provides a haven for terrorist training. We have arrested or killed some of the top leaders of Al-Qaeda. Iran is under great pressure from moderate elements in their society. More moderate Palestinians are challenging Arafat. Pakistani President General Pervez Musharraf is closing down some of the radical schools and mosques that breed fundamentalism. We are having honest discussions with the Saudis about their involvement in promoting Islamic fundamentalism. We may hold back additional aid to Egypt to protest anti-democratic actions taken by the Egyptian government. A quick and decisive victory in any war in Iraq could bring about the first democratic Arab state. The U.S. has created a Global Communications Office to help enhance our image across the world. And the House of Representatives recently approved money on cultural and informational programs targeted at Muslim countries to counter anti-American messages of hate.

At home, flags fly everywhere and there is a new appreciation for the police, firefighters, the armed forces, and others who put their lives on the line for us. Volunteerism and government service is at an all-time high. Our scientists are working on new and effective vaccines to fight biological attacks. New laws are putting the squeeze on financing terrorist operations. There is better cooperation between the various governmental agencies fighting terrorism.

We will prevail in this conflict. Throughout history, free men have always prevailed over those who favor tyranny and oppression. As we face this new evil, we need to recognize it for what it is and be willing to make the sacrifices to defeat it. We are not alone in this struggle. The free people of the world are being tested. With persistence, patience, and collective effort, we will pass this test.

As President Bush stated on September 20, 2001:

> The course of this conflict is not known, yet its outcome is certain...we'll meet violence with patient justice, assured of the right-

ness of our cause and confident of the victories to come…. We will rally the world to this cause by our efforts, by our courage. We will not tire, we will not falter and we will not fail.

There has been and always will be evil in the world. Help fight the evil in this historic conflict and you will learn first hand how one person can change the world. Together, as a Nation, and for all humanity, we will prevail over evil and ensure a good life for our children. That is what it's all about.

Appendix A

Disaster Planning and Supplies

The following information is made available and developed by the Federal Emergency Management Agency and the American Red Cross. To get copies of American Red Cross Community Disaster Education materials, or to find out about registering for a first aid or CPR course, contact your local Red Cross chapter.

A. *Family Disaster Planning—Four Steps to Safety*

1. Find Out What Could Happen to You

- Contact your local Red Cross chapter, local fire department or emergency management office before a disaster occurs—be prepared to take notes.

- Ask what types of disasters are most likely to happen. Request information on how to prepare for each.

- Learn about your community's warning signals: what they sound like and what you should do when you hear them.

- Ask about animal care after a disaster. Animals are not allowed inside emergency shelters because of health regulations.

- Find out how to help elderly or disabled persons, if needed.

- Find out about the disaster plans at your workplace, your children's school or day care center, and other places where your family spends time.

2. Create a Disaster Plan

- Meet with your family and discuss why you need to prepare for disaster. Explain the various dangers that are most likely to happen. Explain what to do in each case.

- Pick two places to meet:
  1. Right outside your home in case of a sudden emergency, like a fire.
  2. Outside your neighborhood in case you can't return home. Everyone must know the address and phone number of the gathering place.

- Ask an out-of-state friend to be your "family contact." After a disaster, it's often easier to call long distance. Other family members should call this person and tell them where they are. Everyone must know your contact's phone number.

- Discuss what to do in an evacuation. Plan how to take care of your pets.

3. Complete This Checklist

- Post emergency telephone numbers by phones (fire, police, ambulance, etc.).

- Teach children how and when to call 9-1-1 or your local Emergency Medical Services number for emergency help.

- Show each family member how and when to turn off the utilities (water, gas, and electricity) at the main switches.

- Check if you have adequate insurance coverage.

- Show each family member where the fire extinguisher (ABC type) is kept, and get training from the fire department on how to use it.

- Install smoke detectors on each level of your home, especially near bedrooms.

- Conduct a home search for all types of hazards.

- Stock emergency supplies and assemble a Disaster Supplies Kit.

- Take a Red Cross first aid and CPR class.

- Determine the best escape routes from your home. Find two ways out of each room.

- Find the safe places in your home for each type of disaster.

4. Practice and Maintain Your Plan

- Quiz your kids every six months or so.

- Conduct fire and emergency evacuations.

- Replace stored water and stored food every six months.

- Test and recharge your fire extinguisher(s) according to manufacturer's instructions.

- Test your smoke detectors monthly and change the batteries at least once a year.

B. *Emergency Communications*

1. Create an emergency communications plan.

Make sure every household member has a contact number to call in the event of an emergency. Include each other's e-mail addresses and telephone numbers (home, work, pager, and cell). Leave these contact numbers at your children's schools and at your workplace. Your family should know that if telephones are not working, use a cell phone or a third party like an out-of-town contact your family knows well to check on each other should a disaster occur. Your selected contact should live far enough away that they would be unlikely to be directly affected by the same event, and they should know they are the chosen contact.

2. Establish a meeting place.

Having a predetermined meeting place away from your home will save time and minimize confusion should your home be affected or the area evacuated. You may even want to make arrangements to stay with a family member or friend in case of an emergency. Be sure to include any pets in these plans.

3. Assemble a disaster supplies kit.

If you need to evacuate your home or are asked to "shelter in place," having some essential supplies on hand will make you and your family more comfortable. Prepare a disaster supplies kit in an easy-to-carry container such as a duffel bag or small plastic trash can. See below for a detailed Disaster Supply Kit. It is also a good idea to include some cash and copies of important family documents (birth certificates, passports, and licenses) in your kit. Copies of essential documents—like powers of attorney, birth and marriage certificates, insurance policies, life insurance beneficiary designations, and a copy of your will—should also be kept in a safe location outside your home. A safe deposit box or the home of a friend or family member who lives out of town is a good choice.

4. Check the school emergency plan.

You need to know if they will they keep children at school until a parent or designated adult can pick them up or send them home on their own. Be sure that the school has updated information about how to reach parents and responsible caregivers to arrange for pickup. Ask what type of authorization the school may require to release a child to someone you designate, if you are not able to pick up your child. During times of emergency the school telephones may be overwhelmed with calls.

5. Get your neighbors involved.

Working with neighbors can save lives and property. Meet with your neighbors to plan how the neighborhood could work together after a disaster until help arrives. If you're a member of a neighborhood organization, such as a home association or crime watch group, introduce disaster preparedness as a new activity. Know your neighbors' special skills (e.g., medical, technical) and consider how you could help neighbors who have special needs, such as disabled and elderly persons. Make plans for childcare in case parents can't get home.

C. <u>Disaster Planning</u>

If disaster strikes:

- Remain calm and be patient.

- Follow the advice of local emergency officials.

- Listen to your battery-powered radio or television for news and instructions.

- If the disaster occurs near you, check for injuries. Give first aid and get help for seriously injured people.

- If the disaster occurs near your home while you are there, check for damage using a flashlight. Do not light matches or candles or turn on electrical switches. Check for fires, fire hazards and other household hazards. Sniff for gas leaks, starting at the water heater. If you smell gas or suspect a leak, turn off the main gas valve, open windows, and get everyone outside quickly.

- Shut off any other damaged utilities.

- Confine or secure your pets.

- Call your family contact—do not use the telephone again unless it is a life-threatening emergency.

- Check on your neighbors, especially those who are elderly or disabled.

1. Evacuation

If local authorities ask you to leave your home, they have a good reason to make this request and you should heed the advice immediately. Listen to your radio or television and follow the instructions of local emergency officials. Keep these simple tips in mind:

1. Wear long-sleeved shirts, long pants and sturdy shoes so you can be protected as much as possible.

2. Take your Disaster Supplies Kit.

3. Take your pets with you; do not leave them behind.

4. Lock your home.

5. Have sufficient cash.

6. Use travel routes specified by local authorities—don't use shortcuts because certain areas may be impassable or dangerous.

7. Stay away from downed power lines.

8. If you're sure you have time:

    • Call your family contact to tell them where you are going and when you expect to arrive.

    • Shut off water and electricity before leaving, if instructed to do so. Leave natural gas service ON unless local officials advise you otherwise. You may need gas for heating and cooking, and only a professional can restore gas service in your home once it's been turned off. In a disaster situation it could take weeks for a professional to respond.

2. Shelter in place

If you are advised by local officials to "shelter in place," what they mean is for you to remain inside your home or office and protect yourself there. Close and lock all windows and exterior doors. Turn off all fans, heating and air conditioning systems. Close the fireplace damper. Get your Disaster Supplies Kit, and make sure the radio is working. Go to an interior room without windows that's above ground level. In the case of a chemical threat, an aboveground location is preferable because some chemicals are heavier than air, and may seep into basements even if the windows are closed. Using duct tape, seal all cracks around the door and any vents into the room. Keep listening to your radio or television until you are told all is safe or you are told to evacuate. Local officials may call for evacuation in specific areas at greatest risk in your community.

D. *First Aid Primer*

If you encounter someone who is injured, apply the emergency action steps: Check-Call-Care. Check the scene to make sure it is safe for you to approach. Then check the victim for unconsciousness and life-threatening conditions. Someone who has a life-threatening condition, such as not breathing or severe bleeding, requires immediate care by trained responders and may require treatment by medical professionals. Call out for help. There are some steps that you can take to care for someone who is hurt, but whose injuries are not life threatening.

Control Bleeding

- Cover the wound with a dressing, and press firmly against the wound (direct pressure).
- Elevate the injured area above the level of the heart if you do not suspect that the victim has a broken bone.
- Cover the dressing with a roller bandage.
- If the bleeding does not stop:
  - Apply additional dressings and bandages.
  - Use a pressure point to squeeze the artery against the bone.
- Provide care for shock.

Care for Shock

- Keep the victim from getting chilled or overheated.
- Elevate the legs about 12 inches (if broken bones are not suspected).
- Do not give food or drink to the victim.

Tend to Burns

- Stop the burning by cooling the burn with large amounts of water.

- Cover the burn with dry, clean dressings or cloth.

Care for Injuries to Muscles, Bones, and Joints

- Rest the injured part.

- Apply ice or a cold pack to control swelling and reduce pain.

- Avoid any movement or activity that causes pain.

- If you must move the victim because the scene is becoming unsafe, try to immobilize the injured part to keep it from moving.

- Listen to local radio and television reports for the most accurate information from responsible governmental and medical authorities on what's happening and what actions you will need to take.

Reduce Any Care Risks

The risk of getting a disease while giving first aid is extremely rare. However, to reduce the risk even further:

- Avoid direct contact with blood and other body fluids.

- Use protective equipment, such as disposable gloves and breathing barriers.

- Thoroughly wash your hands with soap and water immediately after giving care.

Disaster Supplies Kit

There are six basics you should stock for your home: water, food, first aid supplies, clothing and bedding, tools and emergency supplies, and special items. Keep the items that you would most likely need during an evacuation in an easy-to-carry container—suggested items are marked with an asterisk (*). Possible containers include a large, covered trash container, a camping backpack, or a duffle bag.

Water

- Store water in plastic water bottles. Avoid using containers that will decompose or break, such as milk cartons or glass bottles. A normally active person needs to drink at least two quarts of water each day. Hot environments and intense physical activity can double that amount. Children, nursing mothers, and ill people will need more.

- Store one gallon of water per person per day.

- Keep at least a three-day supply of water per person (two quarts for drinking, two quarts for each person in your household for food preparation/sanitation).*

Food

- Store at least a three-day supply of non-perishable food. Select foods that require no refrigeration, preparation or cooking, and little or no water. If you must heat food, pack a can of sterno. Select food items that are compact and lightweight. Include a selection of the following foods in your Disaster Supplies Kit:

  - Ready-to-eat canned meats, fruits, and vegetables

  - Canned juices

  - Staples (salt, sugar, pepper, spices, etc.)

  - High energy foods

- Vitamins
- Food for infants
- Comfort/stress foods

First Aid Kit

Assemble a first aid kit for your home and one for each car.

- Sterile adhesive bandages in assorted sizes
- Assorted sizes of safety pins
- Cleansing agent/soap
- Latex gloves (2 pairs)
- Sunscreen
- 2-inch sterile gauze pads (4-6)
- 4-inch sterile gauze pads (4-6)
- Triangular bandages (3)
- Non-prescription drugs
- 2-inch sterile roller bandages (3 rolls)
- 3-inch sterile roller bandages (3 rolls)
- Scissors
- Tweezers
- Needle
- Moistened towelettes
- Antiseptic

- Thermometer

- Tongue blades (2)

- Tube of petroleum jelly or other lubricant

- Filter Mask (N95 Rating)

Non-Prescription Drugs

- Aspirin or nonaspirin pain reliever

- Anti-diarrhea medication

- Antacid (for stomach upset)

- Syrup of Ipecac (use to induce vomiting if advised by the Poison Control Center)

- Laxative

- Activated charcoal (use if advised by the Poison Control Center)

Tools and Supplies

- Mess kits, or paper cups, plates, and plastic utensils*

- Battery-operated radio and extra batteries*

- Flashlight and extra batteries*

- Cash or traveler's checks, change*

- Non-electric can opener, utility knife*

- Fire extinguisher: small canister ABC type

- Tube tent

- Pliers

- Tape

- Compass

- Matches in a waterproof container

- Aluminum foil

- Plastic storage containers

- Signal flare

- Paper, pencil

- Needles, thread

- Medicine dropper

- Shut-off wrench, to turn off household gas and water

- Whistle

- Plastic sheeting

- Map of the area (for locating shelters)

Sanitation

- Toilet paper, towelettes*

- Soap, liquid detergent*

- Feminine supplies*

- Personal hygiene items*

- Plastic garbage bags, ties (for personal sanitation uses)

- Plastic bucket with tight lid

- Disinfectant

- Household chlorine bleach

Clothing and Bedding

- Include at least one complete change of clothing and footwear per person

- Sturdy shoes or work boots*

- Rain gear*

- Blankets or sleeping bags*

- Hat and gloves

- Thermal underwear

- Sunglasses

Special Items

- Remember family members with special requirements, such as infants and elderly or disabled persons

For Baby*

- Formula

- Diapers

- Bottles

- Powdered milk

- Medications

For Adults*

- Heart and high blood pressure medication

- Insulin

- Prescription drugs

- Denture needs

- Contact lenses and supplies

- Extra eye glasses

Entertainment

- Games and books

Important Family Documents

Keep these records in a waterproof, portable container:

- Will, insurance policies, contracts, deeds, stocks, and bonds

- Passports, social security cards, immunization records

- Bank account numbers

- Credit card account numbers and companies

- Inventory of valuable household goods, important telephone numbers

- Family records (birth, marriage, death certificates)

Appendix B

Additional Resources

A. <u>International Terrorist Organizations</u>

Source: U.S. Department of State

On March 27, 2002, the State Department's list of Foreign Terrorist Organizations (FTOs) was updated to include 33 groups. This partial list focuses on groups recently engaged in terrorist attacks.

- **Abu Sayyaf Group (ASG)** The smallest and most radical of the Islamic separatist groups operating in the southern Philippines. Some ASG members developed ties to the *mujahideen* while fighting in Afghanistan but the group is largely profit-driven. **Activities:** Kidnappings, extortion, murder—in 2001–2002 the group held an American missionary couple and other hostages, several of whom were killed in a shoot-out with Philippine troops.

- **Al-Gama'a al-Islamiyya (Islamic Group, IG)** Egypt's largest militant group, IG's primary goal is to replace Egyptian government with an Islamic state. **Activities:** Armed attacks against Egyptian government officials and Coptic Christians. Launched the 1997 attack at Luxor that killed 58 foreign tourists. Attempted to assassinate Egyptian president Hosni Mubarak in 1995.

- **Al-Jihad/Islamic Egyptian Jihad** Active since the late 1970s, al-Jihad was established to overthrow the Egyptian government and create an Islamic state. Vehemently anti-U.S. and anti-Israel. **Activities:** Armed attacks and car bombings aimed at U.S. and Egyptian facilities. Carried out the 1981 assassination of President Anwar Sadat. Merged with al-Qaeda in June 2001; its leader, Ayman al-Zawahiri, is Osama bin Laden's closest adviser.

- **Al-Qaeda** Established in the late 1980s by Osama bin Laden, al-Qaeda's current stated goals are to drive Americans and American influence out of all Muslim nations, especially Saudi Arabia; destroy Israel; and topple pro-Western dictatorships around the Middle East. Al-Qaeda also aims to unite all Muslims and establish, by force, a global Islamic caliphate. **Activities:** Include the Aug. 1998 bombings of two U.S. embassies in Africa, the Oct. 2000 suicide attack on the U.S.S. *Cole,* the Sept. 2001 attacks on the World Trade Center and Pentagon.

- **Armed Islamic Group (GIA)/Salafi Group for Call and Combat (GSPC)** Extremist group that aims to replace the secular Algerian regime with an Islamic state. **Activities:** Between 1992 and 1998 the group massacred an estimated 100,000 civilians; violence resumed again in 2001.

- **Basque Fatherland and Liberty (ETA)** Spanish separatist group created in 1959 with the aim of establishing an independent Basque homeland. **Activities:** Bombings and assassinations of Spanish government officials.

- **Hamas** Formed in late 1987 to establish an Islamic Palestinian state in place of Israel. Some elements work through mosques and social service institutions. Militant elements advocate and use violence. **Activities:** Many attacks, including suicide bombings, against Israeli civilian and military targets; major force in both intifadas.

- **Harakat ul-Mujahidin (HUM)** Islamic militant group based in Pakistan that operates primarily in Kashmir. The group has been linked to Osama bin Laden and in 1998 called for attacks on the U.S. and Western interests. **Activities:** Attacks against Indian troops, Western tourists, and civilian targets in Kashmir. Hijacked Indian airliner in Dec. 1999 to bargain for release of a number of

Indian-held prisoners, including Ahmad Omar Sheikh, who in July 2002 was sentenced to death for the abduction and murder of U.S. journalist Daniel Pearl.

- **Hezbollah** Extremist Shi'ite group that aims for the creation of Iranian-style Islamic republic in Lebanon. Formed in 1982 after the Israeli invasion of Lebanon, the group is strongly anti-West and anti-Israel. **Activities:** Anti-Israeli and anti-U.S. attacks, including the suicide truck bombing of the U.S. Marine barracks and embassy in Beirut in 1983.

- **Jaish-e-Mohammed (JEM)** Islamic extremist group formed in early 2000 by Masood Azhar, whose release from prison was a condition for the freeing of hostages from an Indian airliner hijacked in Dec. 1999. JEM's overriding objective is Pakistani control of Kashmir. **Activities:** Claimed responsibility for the Oct. 2001 suicide attack on the Kashmir legislative assembly building; implicated, along with Lashkar-e-Tayyiba, in the Dec. 2001 attack on the Indian parliament.

- **Kurdistan Workers' Party (PKK)** Established in 1974 as a Marxist-Leninist insurgent group primarily composed of Turkish Kurds. Seeks an independent Kurdish state in southeast Turkey. **Activities:** Attacks on Turkish diplomatic and commercial facilities in dozens of West European cities in 1993 and 1995. Attacks on tourists and tourist sites.

- **Lashkar-e-Tayyiba (LT)** One of the largest militant groups seeking Pakistani control of Kashmir. **Activities:** Responsible for numerous attacks on Indian military and civilian targets in Kashmir since 1993. Implicated in the Dec. 2001 attack on the Indian Parliament.

- **The Liberation Tigers of Tamil Eelam (LTTE)** The most powerful Tamil group in Sri Lanka. Seeks to create an independent Tamil state. Began its armed conflict with the Sri Lankan government in 1983. **Activities:** Political assassinations of Sri Lankan president Ranasinghe Remadasa in 1993 and Indian prime minister Rajiv

Gandhi in 1991. Massive truck bombings. NOTE: In Feb. 2002, the Sri Lankan government and the Tamil Tigers declared a cease-fire that thus far has held.

- **Mujahedin-e Khalq Organization (MEK/MKO)** An Iranian Marxist-Islamic organization founded in the 1960s. MEK, both anti-Western and against Iran's clerical regime, is bankrolled by Saddam Hussein of Iraq. **Activities:** Murdered dozens of top-level Iranian officials since 1981. Aided Iraqi government in suppression of anti-Hussein Shia and Kurdish uprisings in 1991.

- **The Palestine Islamic Jihad (PIJ)** Loosely affiliated factions committed to the creation of an Islamic Palestinian state and the destruction of Israel through holy war. **Activities:** Suicide bombing attacks against Israeli targets.

- **Popular Front for the Liberation of Palestine (PFLP)** Marxist-Leninist group founded in 1967 by a former PLO member. **Activities:** International terrorist attacks in the 1970s; since then, attacks against Israelis and moderate Arabs; assassination of right-wing Israeli cabinet minister Rehavam Ze'evi in Oct. 2001.

- **Real Irish Republican Army (RIRA)** Launched early in 1998 in protest of Sinn Fein's Sept.1997 adoption of the principles of democracy and non-violence in the pursuit of an all-Irish state; opposed to the Dec. 1999 amendments to the Irish Constitution that retract the Republic's claim to the six northern counties. Composed primarily of members of the 32 County Sovereignty Movement and defectors from the IRA. **Activities:** Bombings, assassinations, and robberies targeting British military and police as well as Protestants in Northern Ireland. Considered responsible for the Aug.1998 car bombing in Omagh, Northern Ireland, and attacks on the British mainland, such as the 2001 bombing of MI6 headquarters in London.

- **Revolutionary Armed Forces of Colombia (FARC)** Best-trained and best-equipped guerrilla organization in Colombia. Established in 1964 as military wing of Colombian Communist Party, seeks to overthrow the government. Anti-U.S. since its inception. **Activities:** Armed attacks against Colombian political and military targets. Traffics in drugs.

- **Revolutionary People's Struggle (ELA)** Extreme leftist group that developed out of the opposition to the military junta that ruled Greece from 1967 to 1974. Self-described revolutionary, anticapitalist, and anti-imperialist group that is strongly anti-U.S. and seeks the removal of U.S. military forces from Greece. **Activities:** Bombings against Greek government and economic targets as well as U.S. military and business facilities. Claimed joint responsibility (with terrorist group 1 May) for more than 20 bombings in 1991.

- **Sendero Luminoso (Shining Path, or SL)** Formed by Maoist professor Abimael Guzman in the late 1960s. Seeks to replace Peruvian institutions with a communist peasant revolutionary regime. **Activities:** One the most ruthless terrorist groups in the West, SL has killed about 30,000 people since 1980. Although the Shining Path waned during the 1990s it has begun a regroup since 2000.

B. <u>State-Sponsored Terrorism</u>

The U.S. State Department has designated the following countries state sponsors of international terrorism: Cuba, Iran, Iraq, Libya, North Korea, Sudan, and Syria. Though most no longer engage directly in terrorist activity themselves, they may support terrorist groups by providing funding or arms. In 2002, President Bush singled out Iran, Iraq, and North Korea for special condemnation, labeling them "an axis of evil."

C. <u>Legislation Regarding Terrorism</u>

- <u>HR2882</u>: Public Safety Officer Benefits bill

- <u>HR2883</u>: Intelligence Authorization Act for Fiscal Year 2002

- HR2884: Victims of Terrorism Relief Act of 2001

- HR2888: 2001 Emergency Supplemental Appropriations Act for Recovery from and Response to Terrorist Attacks on the United States

- HR2926: Air Transportation Safety and System Stabilization Act

- HR3162: Uniting and Strengthening America by Providing Appropriate Tools Required to Intercept and Obstruct Terrorism (USA PATRIOT ACT) Act of 2001

- HR3275: Terrorist Bombings Convention Implementation Act of 2001

- HR3448: Bioterrorism Response Act of 2001

- HR3525: Enhanced Border Security and Visa Entry Reform Act of 2002

- HR3986: To extend the period of availability of unemployment assistance under the Robert T. Stafford Disaster Relief and Emergency Assistance Act in the case of victims of the terrorist attacks of September 11, 2001.

- H.J.Res. 71: Designating September 11 as Patriot Day

- S1372: Export-Import Bank Reauthorization Act of 2002

- S1424: A bill to amend the Immigration and Nationality Act to provide permanent authority for the admission of "S" visa non-immigrants.

- S1438: National Defense Authorization Act for Fiscal Year 2002

- S1447: Aviation and Transportation Security Act

- <u>S1465</u>: A bill to authorize the President to exercise waivers of foreign assistance restrictions with respect to Pakistan through September 30, 2003, and for other purposes.

- <u>S1573</u>: Afghan Women and Children Relief Act of 2001

- <u>S1793</u>: Higher Education Relief Opportunities for Students Act of 2001

- <u>S2431</u>: Mychal Judge Police and Fire Chaplains Public Safety Officers' Benefit Act of 2002

- <u>S.J.Res. 22</u>: A joint resolution expressing the sense of the Senate and House of Representatives regarding the terrorist attacks launched against the United States on September 11, 2001.

- <u>S.J.Res. 23</u>: Authorization for Use of Military Force

D. <u>Useful Sites</u>

- **How to talk to your kids about terrorist attacks**

  <u>http://www.parentcenter.com/refcap/parenting/raising/34843.html</u>

- **Dealing with Children and the After Effects of Terrorism**

  <u>http://www.nhfostercare.org/terrorism.htm</u>

- **The National Center for Children Exposed to Violence (NCCEV)**

  <u>http://www.nccev.org/resources/terrorism/aftermath_index.html</u>

- **The Federation of American Scientists** <u>http://fas.org/irp/crs/</u>

- **Advisory Panel to Assess Domestic Response Capabilities for Terrorism Involving Weapons of Mass Destruction (Gilmore Commission)** http://www.rand.org/nsrd/terrpanel

- **Public War on Terrorism** (U.S. Central Intelligence Agency)

  http://www.cia.gov/terrorism/index.html

- **Al Qaeda Training Manual** http://www.usdoj.gov/ag/trainingmanual.htm

- **America's War against Terrorism: World Trade Center/Pentagon Terrorism and the Aftermath** (University of Michigan Library. Documents Center) http://www.lib.umich.edu/govdocs/usterror.html

- **Annotated Bibliography of Government Documents Related to the Threat of Terrorism & the Attacks of September 11, 2001** (Kevin D. Motes, Oklahoma Department of Libraries) http://www.odl.state.ok.us/usinfo/terrorism/911.htm

- **The Campaign Against International Terrorism: Prospects After the Fall of the Taliban** (Great Britain. House of Commons)

  http://www.parliament.uk/commons/lib/research/rp2001/rp01-112.pdf

- **Countering Terrorism and Protecting Our Forces** (U.S. Department of Defense) http://www.defenselink.mil/other_info/terrorism.html

- **Counterterrorism Office** (U.S. Department of State) http://www.state.gov/s/ct/

- **Documents on Terrorism** (Yale Law School. Avalon Project)

  http://www.yale.edu/lawweb/avalon/terrorism/terror.htm

- **Patterns of Global Terrorism** (U.S. Department of State) http://www.state.gov/s/ct/rls/pgtrpt/

- **Response to Terrorism** (United States Information Agency (USIA))

  http://usinfo.state.gov/topical/pol/terror/

- **September 11 & Terrorism** (Transnational Foundation for Peace and Future Research) **http://www.transnational.org/links/Sept11_terror.html**

- **Terrorism: Questions and Answers** (Council on Foreign Relations)

  http://www.terrorismanswers.com/home/

- **Terrorism Research Center** **http://www.terrorism.com/index.shtml**

- **UN Action against Terrorism** http://www.un.org/terrorism/

- **World Terrorist Attacks and Organizations** (Washington Post)

  http://www.washingtonpost.
  com/wp-dyn/world/issues/terrordata/

- **Terrorism** (Federal Emergency Management Agency (FEMA))

  http://www.fema.gov/hazards/terrorism/terror.shtm

- **Countering the Changing Threat of International Terrorism** (U.S. National Commission on Terrorism) **http://w3.access.gpo.gov/nct/**

- **National Strategy Against Terrorism: Using Weapons of Mass Destruction** (Lawrence Livermore National Laboratory)

  http://www.llnl.gov/str/Imbro.html

- **Office of Homeland Security** (U.S. Office of the President)

  http://www.whitehouse.gov/homeland

- **Response to September 11, 2001 Terrorist Attacks** (Center For Democracy And Technology (CDT)) **http://www.cdt. org/security/010911response.shtml**

- **Special TRAC Report: Criminal Enforcement against Terrorists** (Syracuse University. Transactional Records Access Clearinghouse)

  http://trac.syr.edu/tracreports/terrorism/report011203.html

- **Task Force on Terrorism and the Law—Report and Recommendations on Military Commissions** (American Bar Association) **http://www.abanet.org/leadership/military.pdf**

- **Terrorism and Violent Crime Section** (U.S. Department of Justice)

  http://www.usdoj.gov/criminal/tvcs.html

- **Terrorism Considerations in the Transportation of Spent Nuclear Fuel and High-Level Radioactive Waste** (U.S. Nuclear Regulatory Commission. Nuclear Waste Project Office)

  http://www.state.nv.us/nucwaste/yucca/terrfact.htm

- **Terrorism in a Nuclear Age** (Los Alamos National Laboratory) **http://set.lanl. gov/programs/cif/Curriculum/Terrorism/terrmain.htm**

- **Terrorism in the United States** (U.S. Department of Justice. FBI)

  http://www.fbi.gov/publications/terror/terroris.htm

- **September 11th Sourcebooks** (National Security Archives) **http://www.gwu.edu/~nsarchiv/NSAEBB/NSAEBB55/ index1.html**

- **U.S. Air Force Terrorism Page** (U.S. Air Force Air War College)

  http://www.au.af.mil/au/awc/awcgate/cps-terr.htm

- **U.S. Policy on Combating Terrorism, Unclassified Abstract of Presidential Decision Directive (PDD) 39**

  http://www.fas.org/irp/offdocs/pdd39.htm

- **Counter Terrorism** (EPA Chemical Emergency Preparedness and Prevention Office (CEPPO))

  http://www.epa.gov/ceppo/cntr-ter.html

- **National Terrorism Preparedness Training** (St. Petersburg College. Southeastern Public Safety Institute) **http://terrorism.spjc.edu/**

- **Biologic Terrorism—Responding to the Threat** (U.S. Department of Health and Human Services. Centers for Disease Control and Prevention)

  http://www.cdc.gov/ncidod/EID/vol3no2/downruss.htm

- **Biological and Chemical Weapons** (U.S. Department of Health and Human Services. National Library of Medicine)

  http://www.nlm.nih.gov/medlineplus/biologicalandchemicalweapons.html

- **Biological Warfare** (National Library of Medicine)

  http://www.sis.nlm.nih.gov/Tox/biologicalwarfare.htm

- **Bioterrorism Threat: A Health Spotlight Special Report** (Public Broadcasting Corporation. MacNeil-Lehrer Productions)

  http://www.pbs.org/newshour/health/bioterrorism.html

- **Industrial Chemicals and Terrorism: Human Health Threat Analysis, Mitigation and Prevention** (U.S. Department of Health and Human Services. Centers for Disease Control and Prevention. Agency for Toxic Substances and Disease Registry (ATSDR))

  http://www.techstuff.com/terror/terror.htm

- **Public Health Emergency Preparedness and Response** (U.S. Department of Health and Human Services. Centers for Disease Control and Prevention (CDC)) **http://www.bt.cdc.gov/**

- **Islamic Studies, Islam, Arabic, and Religion** (Professor Alan Godlas, Department of Religion, University of Georgia) **http://www.arches.uga.edu/~godlas/**

- **Muslim Life In America** (U.S. Department of State. Office of International Information Programs)

  http://usinfo.state. gov/products/pubs/muslimlife/homepage.htm

- **Research & Reference Resources: Events of September 11, 2001** (Gary Price) **http://www.freepint.com/gary/91101.html**

- **Terrorism—Background and Threat Assessments** (Federation of American Scientists) **http://www.fas.org/irp/threat/terror.htm**

- **CQ Press Recent Terrorism Events: Background and Context** **http://www.cqpress.com/context**

- **Documenting the Tragedy: Organizational Documentation Projects** (New York State Historical Records Advisory Board) **http://www.nyshrab.org/WTC/projects.html**

- **The Counter Terrorism Page**: **http://www.terrorism.net/index.php?menu=1**

- **FBI field offices**: **http://www.fbi.gov/contact/fo/info.htm**

- **America's War Against Terrorism Document Center**: **http://lib.umich.edu/govdocs/usterror.html**

E. National & International Press Sites

- **Al-Ahram Weekly Online**—Egypt **http://www.ahram.org.eg/ weekly/**

- **BBC Online**—Great Britain **http://www.bbc.co.uk/**

- **Cable News Network (CNN)** **http://www.cnn.com/**

- **Daily Star**—Lebanon **http://www.dailystar.com.lb/**

- **Dawn**—Pakistan **http://www.dawn.com/**

- **International Herald Tribune**—Europe **http://www.iht.com/ frontpage.htm**

- **Jerusalem Post**—Israel **http://www.jpost.com/**

- **Outlook India** **http://www.outlookindia.com/**

- **Times of India** **http://www.timesofindia.com/**

- **National Public Radio (NPR)** **http://www.npr.org/**

- **New York Times** **http://www.nytimes.com/**

- **Public Broadcasting Service** **http://www.pbs.org/**

- **Christian Science Monitor** **http://www.csmonitor.com/**

- **Washington Post** **http://www.washingtonpost.com/**

- **LA Times** **http://www.latimes.com/**

F. Miscellaneous Material

- Newsweek Magazine of October 15, 2001: *"Why They Hate Us: The Roots of Islamic Rage and What We Can Do About It."*

- Inside Terrorism by Bruce Hoffman, Columbia University Press.

- Al-Qaeda: Brotherhood of Terror by Paul Williams, Alpha Publishing.

- The New Terrorism by Walter Laqueur, Oxford University Press.

- Fighting Terrorism by Benjamin Netanyahu, Farrar, Straus and Giroux

- Why Terrorism Works by Alan Dershowitz, Yale University Press

- Longitudes and Attitudes: Exploring the World After September 11 by Thomas Friedman, Farrar, Straus and Giroux.

0-595-26398-4